Ponytail Tales

Ponytail Tales

Barry Matthews

Paris Tokyo New York London Rome Barcelona
Brussels Sydney Berlin & Odd Job

Dani

About the author

Barry Matthews went on a number of school trips in Europe as a boy, long before becoming a Spanish teacher in an English Girls' school and leading similar trips himself. Trips abroad with school friends are the most memorable and fun when the unexpected always happens.

Introduction

A truly inspirational guide to world exploration told in playful language. Ponytail Tales, Paris, Tokyo, New York, London, Rome, Barcelona, Brussels and Sydney are short stories in verse, recording the travels and adventures of a group of girls, known as the Ponytails, from Boden Hall School. These records have been expertly pieced together from recently discovered documents found around the world as well as from school files, personal diaries, letters home, notes and graffiti. Unfortunately, some of the original papers were found in poor condition and not as many of these rare documents have survived as well as we would have liked and sadly a little detail has been lost resulting in some small gaps in our knowledge. It has only been possible to verify the name of one Ponytail for example, Catherine, although we were able to confirm Miss Balard was the teacher who led all the groups on trips for the school's mysterious benefactor, the Lady Boden. The stories help to introduce the excitement of world cities as well as their languages and attractions. The first ever trip is to Paris where the group of Ponytails see the sights and meet local characters and their many pets as well as brushing with the native wildlife, visiting markets and trying the local food. As far as we have been able to tell, after exploring the Ponytails would habitually return home to Boden Hall for a traditional pillow fight before settling down to swot and plan their next adventure. In the county of Shropshire quite close to Wales is the school where we find our Ponytail Tales; where the Lady Boden would've never stinted to get these tales restored and printed. If only our records were a bit clearer so we could get a bit nearer to knowing what really went on, but this is what we have right or wrong. By restoring these papers, it has been possible to create an invaluable travel companion for young people one story at a time. Please remember our good intentions and forgive the errors and imperfections. If chronicle of fact or just a rhyme the truth is lost in the mists of time. More documentation is always being discovered and although it is not possible to hurry the restoration processes, it may be possible to present more Ponytail Tales in the future.

For some time, restorers and researchers have been pulling additional restored documents to one side as they could not confirm the exact location of these events with any certainty. These documents have been stored in a separate archive in the Office for Doubtful Documents under the title, "Odd Job". Although it has not always been possible to verify the locations it has now been decided to place these records alongside the Ponytail Tales as it is considered likely they at least happened at the same time as the Ponytails' travels.

Regarding our team of tireless restorers, perhaps we should stand to show our appreciation or possibly make some small donation. But then, they all knew when they started this was no job for the faint-hearted and they knew your review would be overflowing and that's all they need to keep 'em going. Thank you for your consideration.

Paris

This Ponytail Tale was found by chance
In a railway buffet in deepest France.
Left in haste by an unsettled bill
Exactly where's a mystery still.

These pages were found jumbled and rumpled
Unwanted, creased and crumpled.
Then experts with ink and glue
Fixed 'em up as good as new.

It may have been all go and pressure
With sticky fingers stuck together.
And inky spots and inky spurts
Running down inky shirts.

But everyone knew when they started
This was no job for the faint-hearted.
They knew your review would be glowing
And that's what kept 'em going.

Miss Balard led the group
Fuelled on *croûtons* and onion soup.
Banks left and right to reconnoitre
A nibbled *baguette* for her pointer.

The Ponytails found a *café* table
With a wonky leg and unstable.
A summer breeze stole Miss Balard's hat
And dropped it where the Ponytails sat.

It could've soared like a glider
If the brim had been a bit wider.
Under the leg they folded the hat
And continued with their chit chat.

In this old *café* covered in vines
Sat the Ponytails in two straight lines.
But after taking a second look
That should be in another book.

In the *Marché aux Puces* a shopping spree
For the Ponytails to see what they could see.
The Ponytails found a bizarre buy
A Boden Hall old school tie.

The Ponytails found another bargain
A special offer in market jargon.
The Mona Lisa without a frame
And two more out back just the same.

Another picture they looked at
Was Napoleon in a big hat.
The portrait had been in the wars
For ten *euros* it could be yours.

The emperor's trousers were among the junk
They're very small they must've shrunk.
Just a little tear and a rip
But nothing wrong with the zip.

In a glass case was a stuffed trout
Pouting because it couldn't get out.
Let's make a copy of the key
And when no one's looking set him free.

There's pullovers and jumpers in every size
But the Ponytails soon realise,
A pashmina, cashmere or mohair sweater
Always fits the goats better.

An old picture postcard collection
Showed regions from every direction.
With areas exposed, bleak and barer
And some parts even rarer.

The Ponytails found trumpets and a trombone
It's a long time since they'd been blown.
And a saxophone and two bassoons
There must be a way to blow up balloons.

On the *métro* two mice were running along live rails
Watched by the Ponytails.
But the current from the mains
Can rattle mice as well as trains.

The mice were wondering what if
They were shocked and tossed skew-whiff.
What if they were flung high and scatty
Landing befuddled and head scratchy?

On the Paris *métro* there are scary moments
Some for us and some for rodents.
But there's nothing like a piece of cheese
To put anxious mice at ease.

Monsieur *Clochard* was sleeping on a bench
After lunch, he was very French.
He saved some *fromage* for the mice
He's done that before once or twice.

Quasimodo lived up a bell tower
And swung on the bells every hour.
A little-known fact about this Quasi chap
Is he liked to swing, sing and clap.

Quasimodo's boyish charm
Was the talk of *Notre Dame*.
Quasimodo listened to the choir
And joined in, he was a trier.

Look at me on my bell
You'd like to too I can tell.
Ding dong bing bong
But we can't all get on.

Quasimodo and it's official
Could tap his feet but couldn't whistle.
Singing and swinging in and out of tune
Raging and howling at the moon.

The Ponytails visited the *Musée des Égouts*
That's the sewers to me and you.
What could go wrong?
What a whiff what a pong.

Two lady rat trappers on their first day
Weren't going to let a rat get away.
A rat was scratching his ear
Not in the trap but very near.

The rat sniffed the bait
And stepped inside was it too late?
Oh, no! it's Ratatouille
He prefers something chewy.

The rat wouldn't eat that yuk
The trappers had no beginner's luck.
The Ponytails wondered what more was hid
Beneath that Paris manhole lid.

The *Louvre* always closes on the dot
You must be quick to see the lot.
The Ponytails saw the *Mona Lisa* or *Gioconda*
To see them both would've taken longer.

And noticed as they looked a while
How the security guard had her smile.
And soon became aware
Of how he had the same hair.

It's not only that but just a little more
That they may not have noticed heretofore.
Like how he's always seated in her pose
And likes to dress in the same clothes.

And they may not have missed
How his right hand holds his left wrist.
He was very keen on his Lisa beauty
And stared all day on and off duty.

A French poodle had one aim
Fifi La Grande was her name.
To have the most exclusive *coiffeur*
Cut and style her curly fur.

Clipped, dipped and flossed
Tagged and chipped so she wouldn't get lost.
And massaged to release the tension
Deloused too which is worth a mention.

Sniffing and snorting as if for rabbits
Fifi had some funny habits.
Excusez-moi I know I slobber
Do you like my new collar?

Haute couture or *haute cuisine*
Fifi wasn't sure what they mean.
I don't know what to do
Should I wear it or should I chew?

In the *fête de la musique*
Miss Ballard's shoes began to squeak.
All went well until by chance
A Parisian asked Miss Balard to dance.

He said come closer *chérie*, he wouldn't bight 'er
She really should've held on tighter.
A right foot here and left foot back
She hit the floor with a smack.

Unable to stand or even sit
She tried to look as if she'd meant it.
Miss Balard couldn't go another inch
And then her shoes began to pinch.

Oh no! what a disaster
Lucky, she had a sticky plaster.
But she never used up the lot
She kept one back for a spot.

Ponytails love *croissants* hot from the oven
Twelve at least or even a dozen.
With butter and jam who could resist
And chocolate and almonds if you insist.

There's just one left. No, I couldn't
Oh, go on. No, I shouldn't.
Oh, go on be my guest
You've eaten all the rest.

Dunking *croissants* is also fun
But no one wants a soggy one.
It's all very well when you begin
Just don't drop it in.

Remember if it's your first try
Croissant wet fingers dry.
Or there's the Ponytails' technique
Not too shallow not too deep.

A lemony bun was the attraction
For some sugary waspy action.
A wasp came for a share
Why not? it's only fair.

Wasps don't make good pets
The sugarier it is the swarmier it gets.
And was it Voltaire, Sartre or Aristotle
Who said never trap a wasp in a bottle?

That's enough buzzing and humming
It's time to use some animal cunning.
Come on waspy are you in there still?
It's only a bottle not the *Bastille.*

But things got out of hand
More and more came into land.
Swarms swarming out the sun
Landing on that sticky bun.

French can be complex
With accents acute and circumflex.
But the Ponytails use textbooks
So's not to make too many mistooks.

They put the accent where it goes
Speaking French through the nose.
And add a Gallic shrug like a native
With onion and garlic to be creative.

With the books grammatical and phrasal
And fragrant speech shruggy and nasal,
They put the accents where they belong
Got some right and got some wrong.

In Paris you can learn this and more
That's what Paris is for, *alors*.
It's *la vie Parisienne*
It's like that now and it was like that then.

Looking in the *Trocadero Fontaine*
The Ponytails couldn't explain
Why a frog changed direction
To settle on Catherine's reflection.

Or why it tried to make its resting place
On Catherine's bobbing face.
Or why the frog mistook this *anglaise* craft
For a lily pad or drifting raft.

The frog hopped on but just got wetter
Others tried but did no better.
Ponytails and frogs were in confusion
About what's real and what's an illusion.

The Ponytails were confused
About why Catherine's reflection was misused.
But Catherine just bobbed and weaved with a wink
Smiling and waving never to sink.

The Ponytails went up the tower that Eiffel created
It never rusts if you keep it painted.
But there's no ladder high enough
You have to use a very long brush.

The painters can stand on a chair
Or a tin of paint if they dare.
But mustn't disturb or go near
Monsieur Eiffel the engineer.

Monsieur Eiffel has a place in the tower
To go to bed, get up and shower.
He sits on his balcony with a piece of cake
And feeds the birds 'til it gets late.

Monsieur Eiffel has a head for heights
And sleeps outside on warm nights.
He's never troubled by vertigo
And sleeps in the moonshine's glow.

The Ponytails saw the French are inclined
To play bowls to unwind.
The French are very good bowlers
And not bad pitchers and rollers.

The Ponytails had a game of bowls
That's like golf without the holes.
Or *croquet* without the mallet
And tennis without the racket.

In the Luxembourg Gardens a game of *boule*
A Ponytail *forté* as a rule.
Knees bend for an underarm swinger
Like pitching horseshoes for a ringer.

In the Tuileries Gardens a game of *pétanque*
With Ponytails hitting every clonk.
The Ponytails' aim was true
Well played but *déjà vu.*

An eel swam from Cayenne
Across the Sargasso and up the Seine.
Bonjour ma petite amie
I'm back again remember me?

I know I've grown a little longer
And put on weight like a conger.
But shall we swim again around the clock
As we did in that *belle epoch*?

Now my wriggle is a little slow
I've missed Paris' moonlit glow.
Can we pick up the pieces
And wiggle over the river's sandy beaches?

With the banks left and right
Or violin *sérénads* all night.
And wooing on the piano
It's not like that in the Sargasso.

Dashing for a *rendezvous*
Catherine slipped and lost a shoe.
And collided with a souvenir seller
Oh! poor Cinderella.

Now she had to hop
Into that souvenir shop.
And began to stumble and collide
With all those things sold inside.

Posters, trinkets and keyrings
Notepads, charms and things.
The shop was soon depleted
Of so many things they hadn't needed.

A boy de *Londres* was quick witted
Found the shoe and knew who it fitted.
Had she fallen under her lucky star?
A blush a crush. *Ooh là là!*

On the Vincennes Lake a nautical note
The Ponytails hired a little rowboat.
A sailboat past on the starboard side
Coming about, *le capitaine* cried.

Heave to and heave ho
Capsize and over you go.
But they made fast to a willow tree
Worse things happen at sea.

The Ponytails' way wasn't clear
They were facing backwards and the rear.
Rowing is the wrong way round
The Ponytails could run aground.

Directions change and courses alter
On this busy Paris water.
Boats could gybe and boats could tack
Ducks could duck and ducks could quack.

Ice cream and Ponytails go together
Any time any weather.
In Boden Hall hot or nippy
There's always time for a Mr. Whippy.

They don't all play Popeye the Sailor Man
But the Ponytails know an ice cream van.
A vendor's cry began a stampede
Vivre la glâce! they all agreed.

Monsieur's just made a fresh batch
The Ponytails were queuing at the hatch.
Sorbet scoops doubles and singles
Oui Monsieur heavy on the sprinkles.

Lots of flavours but then the *gran* shock
Monsieur's all out of choc.
Strawberry's yours and vanilla's mine
Avez-vous un 99?

Soon their trip would be over
On the train and back to Dover.
Going to Paris was easy-peasy
So, getting back should be peasy-easy.

The Ponytails arrived home just in the nick
For a pillow fight if they were quick.
With feathers flying and shooting alofty
That's no place for a softy.

As night fell over Boden Hall
There was not a sound nothing at all.
It was quiet then but just a mo
With Ponytails you never know.

There'd be time to reminisce
And remember Paris with their favourite Miss.
Soon plans would be made
For a brand-new escapade.

Fin

Tokyo

This Ponytail Tale was found one day
In a waterfront *café* near Tokyo Bay.
Left in haste by an unsettled bill
Exactly where's a mystery still.

These pages were found jumbled and rumpled
Lost, creased and crumpled.
Then experts with ink and glue
Fixed 'em up as good as new.

It may have been all go and pressure
With sticky fingers stuck together.
And inky spots and inky spurts
Running down inky shirts.

It wasn't easy to unjumble the bits and pieces
Fix the wrinkles and smooth the creases.
But our tales are no longer in tatters
And your review is now all that matters.

A *sushi* restaurant had a selection
Of conveyor belt perfection.
Perfect *sushi* to look at
If only it could've stayed like that.

Someone must've pushed a wrong button
Sushi shouldn't move so sudden.
Like a train set going faster and faster
The *sushi* was heading for disaster.

The *sushi* came off the rails
All over the Ponytails.
Sushi has its time and place
That's never in a Ponytail's face.

Sushi gets in a mess
If the rice isn't firmly pressed.
Miss Balard did balancing tricks
Catching rice with chopsticks.

It should be said at this juncture
Only the more experienced dunker.
Should attempt dunking rice in soy sauce
The risks are clear enough of course.

Short grain does the dunking trick
Medium too if it's not too thick.
But long grain's not starchy and sticky
Dunking long grain can be tricky.

Dunking *sushi* isn't for the faint hearted
Many who try wish they'd never started.
Rice can fall apart and go to pieces
With every dunk the risk increases.

It's hard enough with a biscuit
The Ponytails were advised against it.
The risks are too high, let it go
What, stop now? I should coco.

A jumping spider's eyes
Were fixed on dancing flies.
But he was thinking a *gekko japonicus*
Has his eyes on the lot of us.

The spider's jumpy knees
Are common to his species.
But no matter how springy sprung
He didn't have that gecko's tongue.

The flies were quick to disperse
Weak kneed and conflict averse,
The gecko stuck out its tongue
Missed two flies and another one.

It was different when he was young
Tongues were flicked and webs were spun.
A gecko knew where he stood
Spiders couldn't, geckos could.

A wandering songsmith came their way
With the saddest of tunes to play.
The Ponytails said hello with a low bow
Quite low anyhow.

All alone like a single grain of rice
Long grain, to be precise.
Or a lone sampan on the Sea of Japan
Stood this lonely flute tootin' man.

The one to whom he had been plighted
Left him and now his life was blighted.
But the Ponytails could all agree
There's plenty more fish in the sea.

The wandering minstrel gave a toot
On a yellow bamboo flute.
Such a melancholic fellow
Oh, fellow, toot yellow, toot yellow.

This gloomy mood we must conclude
Was nothing but an interlude.
And now in girlhood's happy spring
The Ponytails wanted to sing.

A *karaoke* café was just the place
For a Ponytail change of pace.
Where no one ever fluffs their lines
And no one ever mimes.

Okeydokey
Time for Ponytail *karaoke*.
J-Pop rock and bop
To liven up this music shop.

Karaoke made it easy
If you forget the words it's lemon squeezy.
This was Ponytail heaven
Play it backwards it's squeezy lemon.

The Ponytails found a cosplay chest
And dressed up for the fest.
Catherine was dressed head to toe
In a golden *kimono*.

Draped in silky threads of gold
Like an empress in days of old.
Now she looked like the others
Her hair and costume came in colours.

With a twist and shout as she missed her cue
Catherine tripped and lost a shoe.
But the songs couldn't wait for ever
Oh! poor Cinderella.

Ain't That A Shame
Let's Twist Again.
Magical Mystery Tour
They don't write 'em like that anymore.

A vending machine was selling oodles
Of piping hot slurpy noodles.
But what bad luck
The Ponytails' coin got stuck.

And no amount of pokey pen
Could get the machine to drop the yen.
The Ponytails were in no doubt
They would never get the noodles out.

But rocking up in a Honda or was it a Nissan
Came a gallant salaryman.
Using the edge of his calling card
He released the coin for Miss Ballard.

Saying leave this to me ladies
Now I remember he was in a Mercedes.
Then our Tokyo trouble-shooter
Said *sayonara* and bibbed his hooter.

A blue car and a *rickshaw* had a race
Downhill and in a steep place.
Cars run on oil and stuff
Rickshaws only run on puff.

But this *rickshaw* was over the speed limit
It was going to get a speeding ticket.
No excuses good or poor
Fast or slow the law's the law.

He stuck the ticket on the car for safe keeping
And got on the pavement that's not cheating.
And down a one way for good measure
That's alright he was under pressure.

The *shariki* was fast on slopes
Could he win? he lived in hopes.
But with a false start and if it's hilly
Can a *rickshaw* really beat a car? don't be silly.

In Tokyo there's a *shogun's* army
Made with paper *origami.*
A fold a crease a flap a twist
There's a *ninja* a *samurai* a plucky *sumoist.*

The Ponytails made a paper plane
To start a whose went the furthest game.
And stuck a paperclip on its nose
Where it stops no one knows.

To see how far they could throw
They went up high in Tokyo.
And remember if you're beginners
There're no losers only winners.

Flying planes is an art
It's not the winning it's the taking part.
A victory roll and a swoop
Then back to base to regroup.

Lying in a sudsy Jacuzzi
The Ponytails were feeling snoozy.
A Ponytail forgets her troubles
Soaking in so many bubbles.

But remember if you're having a soaky
And you're feeling safe and soapy.
You never know what you might find
Sneaking up behind.

Uninvited and with wagging tailspin
Soppy dogs came barging in.
Sniffy woofies and hairy barkers
Are all you need when you're starkers

Who left the door open?
When was the lock broken?
Who was the first to shout?
Who let the dogs out?

Before the heights of Mount Fuji
A great wave passed by out at sea.
With three boats in the rise and swell
Or was it four? it's hard to tell.

The wave was pushing with full force
Little boats were knocked off course.
If only this were boating weather
If only they had a propeller.

Then the wave broke
Over the crews of oak.
If only they were closer to the dock
If only this were a picture on woodblock.

Could they carve a safe path home
Through the heavy seas of foam
And reach their native shores
Collapsing exhausted across the oars?

A *sumo* has a chance however slender
To be a champ or a contender.
And even if defeated and worked over
Never loses his composure.

Sumos always look tough
And never get in a tizzy huff.
A *sumo* tough and bulky
Never gets in a big sulky.

Even when steamrollered and outsmarted
A sumo never looks downhearted.
No cold shower or body rub
Could ever make a *sumo* blub.

A *sumo* will always hide
What he's feeling inside.
And never looks a bit on edgy
As you would with that wedgie.

On the subway tube or *chikatetsu*
They'll squash and squeeze you in to
A train that's already packed
With crushed commuters from front to back.

Official pushers push in white gloves
Using pulls pushes and shoves.
And if they can't close the door
They'll push and pull some more.

All the lines are colour coded
And all the trains are overloaded.
But if you all move together
You won't be under so much pressure.

What they say and it must be true
You can't always get off when you want to.
If you want to be sure
Always stand near the door.

Ponytails like to
Write a Japanese *haiku*.
Do you like to too?
I know I do.

Or prune *bonsai* trees
Just like the Japanese.
Every twig and bough
Shaped like a ponytail.

You only go up to nine in *sudoku*
Tens and elevens just won't do.
Nine is the largest figure
So don't try anything bigger.

Nine is an unlucky number in Japan
People avoid it if they can.
Koi are said to be lucky without a doubt
So, nine *koi* must cancel each other out.

The tea ceremony was yet to come
The Ponytails would be mum.
Two bags and one for the pot
Milk in first ready or not.

It was all going so well, until
The Ponytails couldn't pay the bill.
Things got much worse
When Miss Balard forgot her purse.

Let the punishment fit the crime
Though the job would take some time.
Every plate dish and cup
They had to do the washing up.

The Ponytails got going chop-chop
Up to their necks in soapy slop
If the Ponytails had three wishes
There would be far, far. far, fewer dishes.

The Imperial Gardens had ponds of *koi*
Always mouthing their approval and joy.
Free from a world of endless trouble
Or is this joy but a bubble?

A little *koi* was blowing bubbles
Rolling in swirls, gurgles and guggles.
But she went too deep without stopping
And came back up with both ears popping.

The little *koi* who couldn't be littler
Was diving too deep for a tiddler.
The little fish left the shoal
To take a look at the plughole.

When diving in a fountain, pond or pool
She forgot the golden rule.
Like all little fish we might suppose
She forgot to hold her nose.

Some say in the dead of night
When we are tucked up out of sight.
Behind painted screens and sliding doors
Snuggled in futons on wooden floors.

Characters and figures on vase or fan
Begin to move all over Japan.
While the Ponytails were dreaming of home
Far from the Chrysanthemum Throne.

People of old looking quaint
Were coming to life in shiny paint.
And from vase to fan sprang and leapt
While the Ponytails dreamt and slept.

And stories might unfold
About great events in days of old.
When treasons and plots
Came to life on fans and pots.

Across a clear Tokyo sky
A weather balloon was limping by.
Balloons however scientific
May gasp for air over the Pacific.

It once seemed it would last for ever
In Tokyo's settled weather.
But that's what happens in monsoons
Cyclones and typhoons.

It wasn't always as it is now
All crinkled and wrinkled somehow.
Storms would gather and storms would rage
The shrivelled balloon was showing its age.

Returning from a high-level mission
Losing height and condition.
Back at last queasy and wheezy
Glad to be home it hadn't been easy.

The Ponytails would always remember Japan
The flutist and the salaryman.
Memories to last for ever and ever
Till pebbles grow into boulders, which would be clever.

If the Ponytails made a little list
Of all the things they missed.
At the top we might find
That *rickshaw* man not far behind.

Another thing the *Ponītēru* never forgot
Was saying *arigatō* a lot.
Konnichiwa came a close second
Or so the *Ponītēru* reckoned.

After hightailing it home from their globetrot
The Ponytails settled down to swot.
But all work and no play
Was never the Ponytail way.

And now a sort of epilogue
To complete this Ponytail travelogue.
No better way to start the night
Than with a Ponytail pillow fight.

A no holds barred free for all
The usual caper at Boden Hall.
Armed with two pillows in each hand
And swinging like a one-man-band.

The Ponytails biffed and boffed
Said good night and nodded off.
As the Boden Hall clock chimed through the night
The Ponytails slept tighty-tight.

Time enough to reminisce
And remember Tokyo with their favourite Miss.
Soon plans would be laid
For a brand-new escapade.

おしまい

New York

This Ponytail Tale was found one day
In Grand Central USA.
Left in haste by an unsettled bill
Exactly where's a mystery still.

Please remember our good intentions
And forgive the errors and imperfections.
If chronicle of fact or just a rhyme
The truth is lost in the mists of time.

This document was found in a sorry state
Faded and torn you'll appreciate.
But with care and attention to retell the story
The pages were restored to their former glory.

It wasn't easy to unjumble the bits and pieces
Fix the wrinkles and smooth the creases.
But our tales are no longer in tatters
And now your review is all that matters.

The New York streets are under the control
Of the N.Y.P.D. patrol.
A Ponytail must watch her step
Not to be a jaywalking rubberneck.

A mounted policeman passed by at a trot
On a horse whose name he forgot.
Both had the law to enforce
New York's finest and his horse.

What was that horse's name?
No-one remembers what a shame.
It wasn't, Flicka, Flash or Dung
Cor, it's on the tip of my tongue.

The gum chewing New York cop
Whistled and made the traffic stop.
The Ponytails were shown the way
To stay safe and have a nice day.

The new kids on the block
Were in for a linguistic shock.
Toity-toid and toid sounded absoid
The funniest place they ever 'oid.

And hey wadda yer know?
caw-fee is a cup of Joe.
And in a drive thru with an off roader
You can order a slice and soda.

If you're hawngry and headin' to the deli
Remember jam is much the same as jelly.
And if your order is on a hero roll
Yo! you can always get that to go.

But wut's da matta wit da way dey speak?
Nuttin, da New Yawkas are unique.
If you can understand dem dare
You can understand dem anywhere.

Another cop twirled his truncheon
Looking up at the construction
Of a new neon sign
On Times Square's skyline.

Wut's dat? He often mused
Looking up all confused.
And why's it called Times Square
If dare's no square dare?

There's no square it's true
Dat's. I mean that's 7th. Avenue.
And along it come and go
Cops twirling truncheons like a yoyo.

Now he looks more confused
Dat's not a truncheon wut I used.
Dat's a baton or a night stick
Come and watch my twirling trick.

The Empire State Building had a good view
Of the ups and downs on Fifth Avenue.
The Ponytails saw the sights
From those dizzy Manhattan heights.

In the Empire State skyscraper
The lift is used less than the elevator.
Whichever one you decide
It's better than the climb outside.

The elevator drops in free fall
Like a banister slide at Boden Hall.
Top to toe in a New York minute
Even faster with someone in it.

Never one to be outdone
King Kong climbed the greatest climb ever clumb.
Up 102 floors to monkey glory
That really was a very tall storey.

In Central Park a lady balloon seller
Was blown about in bad weather.
With her strings caught in a tangle
Up she went in a New York dangle.

She went high as you'd expect
Just how high no-one checked.
Perhaps higher than a plane or chopper
Higher and higher like a space hopper.

Like a goalie's kick
Bounced once and taken quick.
But no-one there could stop 'er
Like they do in a game of soccer.

But can a rubber ball bouncing willy nilly
Really go higher than a chopper? don't be silly!
What about an astronaut when he's space walking?
Now you're talking.

In Central Park if a lady gets entangled
Helicopters and jets may be scrambled.
But if the pilots were not mistaken
They were being overtaken.

A New York ballooner never quits
Not even upside down doing the splits.
Doing the splits upside down
Like Spiderman the wrong way around.

Then a breezy gust gusted
And many balloons were burst and busted.
After the last pop and bang
The Lady landed where she began.

Back on land and crisis over
She regained her composure.
Just a little achy and shaky.
That's no way to treat a lady.

A Wall Street millionaire
Isn't afraid of bulls or bears.
But would never step on the cracks
That's true that is facts are facts.

Millionaires cross their fingers and touch wood
They'd touch chimney sweeps too if they could.
Lucky heather, shamrock and a black cat
Millionaires love all that.

But it's best to plan in advance
And not leave too much to chance.
It's more to do with the price of gold
And when you bought and when you sold.

On Wall Street Fearless Girl is often likened
To a girl who's never frightened.
But keeps a little lucky charm
That can't do any harm.

In a Harlem basketball game
A fumbled ball was to blame.
For a missed slam dunk
That ball should've been sunk.

And while we're on the subject
A basket ball's not the only object
To be dunked so often and frequent
A biscuit can get the same treatment.

A word on dunkers and the daily hazards they face
You may know about it but just in case.
You're only as good as your last dunk
One drippy bicky and you're sunk.

For New Yorkers dunking a biscuit is very tame
And dunking a cookie is much the same.
New Yorkers wouldn't even make a fuss
About dunkin' donuts, they're not like us.

The Ponytails found a bodega in Queens
But not the biggest by any means.
So full of pastries puff and shortcrust
And cronut and pie dough fit to bust.

The Ponytails threw a pinch of bagel
To a bird under the table.
Not a lot only a smidgen
Just enough for a pigeon.

That's enough you silly bird
That's what they said word for word.
That's what fuhgeddaboudit means
In Brooklyn and Queens.

But the more the Ponytails tried to shoo
The more the flock of pigeons grew.
A pigeon is not so easily put off
When there's bodega bagel to scoff.

In a room scrapping the sky
The Ponytails grabbed some shuteye.
While far below the Manhattan streets
Were full of automobiles hoots and beeps.

And a seagull soared above the East River
But why wasn't her partner with 'er?
Where have you gone my little songbird?
Your squark and shriek are no longer heard.

Could it be something I said
When you pinched my fish head?
You don't have to snap or flap
Over every oily fishy scrap.

Remember those dainty puffins, skewers and plovers
And try to improve your table manners.
Come back soon but without that smell
Of tinned oyster, mussel and cockle shell.

What use is my dainty wingspan
Without a great gull as my wingman?
On land, sea or air
What's the point if you're not there?

I'm not one to nag
But must you eat the chips and bag.
And when you go down the bins
Swallow the sardines not the tins.

I'm not one to go on and on
But must you always smell and pong?
This is the land Columbus discovered
Remember you're a gull not a buzzard.

There's no need to tug and tussle
Over everything you gobble and guzzle.
You're right my dear, what was I thinking?
Now I'm back I'll stop stinking.

A burst fire hydrant near a Downtown drain
Had the Ponytails singing in the rain.
Soon every kid on a brownstone stoop
Joined the Ponytail musical troupe.

The Ponytails were overtaken by pirouettes
Pirouetted by baton twirling majorettes.
A marching band joined in the fun
But the Ponytails weren't to be outdone.

Miss Balard had taught them jazz
Hitting all the right notes, or as near as.
The Ponytails learned it fast
With drums, sax and trumpet blast.

The Ponytails caused a bit of an uproar
For two bits they'd have caused some more.
The world's best whirling, twirling, showbiz kids
Along with Boden Hall's that is.

The Ponytails went for a skateboard ride
Downtown and the Lower East Side.
Skateboarding has only one rule I would say
Never get in the way.

And the Ponytails were soon to find
Using the sidewalk for a crooked grind.
Or likewise for a noseslider
Can stop the board but not the rider.

So many clunks and clonks
Between Queens and The Bronx.
And so many rattles and shakes
The Ponytails couldn't find the brakes.

It's not easy looking cool
Head over heels in a sprawl.
And trying to bail out
With a ponytail flapping about.

Temptation awaited the Ponytails
At Saks, Macy's and Bloomingdale's.
But Miss Balard's group of scholars
Were not so easily parted from their dollars.

Nickels and dimes can buy so much
When shopping for bobby pins and such.
The Ponytails were in luck
A bag full for just a buck.

The Ponytails found a one-stop shop
For Hershey bars and soda pop.
A drugstore open twenty-four-seven
Or was that a 7-Eleven?

After a Ponytail shopping spree
Central Park and a game of Frisbee.
Running and sliding just for fun
Like the Yankees on a home run.

From Manhattan's Lower East Side
The ponytails went for a ghost train ride.
When it comes to ghost trains versions vary
But Coney Island's was really scary.

Full of shakes, shivers and collywobbles
Ghosts, phantoms and demons' squabbles.
Where even the spiders were too scared
To get on board and never dared.

Warning signals and palpitations
Bad feelings and rumbling sensations.
But never rise to the provocation
And never pull the chain in the station.

Doors are slammed and flags are flown
Windows are shut and whistles are blown.
When one door opens another door shuts
Spooks and ghosts going nuts.

New York fountains are never ignored
Flushed, gushed and restored.
Taps turn and water pours
Pumps pump and water soars.

It's been a tradition for so many summers
For joggers and long-distance runners.
For New Yorkers and newcomers
To sing the praises of the plumbers.

If you're an athlete who wants to win
Or a jogger trying to begin
It's nice to pass by and have a look in
And see what it'd be like to have a twin.

Catherine's reflection was caught in the spray
Tinkled and sprinkled and washed away.
Nothing lasts for ever
Oh! poor Cinderella.

The Ponytails left The City's borders
Setting sail for Hudson waters.
Anchored safely by an island quay
Watched over by the Statue of Liberty.

Where Blackfoot, tenderfoot and Crow
Could've made friends with the Arapaho.
Or the Cherokee, Kickapoo and Navajo
You never know.

Perhaps the very place where
Little White Dove met Running Bear.
Where a Mohican brave's tomahawk
Was thrown like kisses across New York.

And where they rode the same pony
Bareback and natives only.
Where together LWD ♡ RB
Carved their initials on a tree.

The Ponytails were catching some rays
Shooting the breeze, happy days.
Kicking back time to chill
And cutting some slack better still.

Miss Balard was surprised
To see Ponytails so Americanised.
Chewing gum and eating apple pie
Hats over eyes for some shuteye.

And raising hats with a playing card
Saying howdy mam to Miss Balard.
Time to hit the trail
And close another Ponytail Tale.

The Ponytails like to chill
And hanging out is better still.
Goofing off is really cool
But it's neat to get back to school.

Now they're home first things first
Time for another pillow burst.
One more swirling woosh
And a kilo of feathers in the mush.

More Ponytails dropped and plummeted
Pommelled, pummelled and buffeted.
More swinging highs and lows
Of bouncing bedding and pillows.

A Ponytail will never retreat
Even when swiped off her feet.
If clobbered, befuddled or upended
She knows the danger is only pretended.

Fair's fair when you've been clouted
The outcome is never really doubted.
It's all in fun you know you'll find
In global tish tosh of this kind.

And now a sort of epilogue
To complete this Ponytail travelogue.
As the Boden Hall clock chimed through the night
They picked up the feathers and turned out the light.

After getting home from their globetrot
The Ponytails settled down to swot.
But all work and no play
Was never the Ponytails' way.

As night fell over Boden Hall
There was not a sound, nothing at all.
It was quiet then but just a mo
With Ponytails you never know.

Time enough to reminisce
And remember New York with their favourite Miss.
Soon plans would be laid
For a brand-new escapade.

End

London

This Ponytail Tale was found yellowed and curly
In a London café bright and early.
Left in haste by an unsettled bill
Exactly where's a mystery still.

In the county of Shropshire quite close to Wales
Is the school where we find our Ponytail Tales.
Where the Lady Boden would've never stinted
To get these tales restored and printed.

This document was found in a sorry state
Faded and torn you'll appreciate.
But with care and attention to retell the story
The pages were restored to their former glory.

It wasn't easy to unjumble the bits and pieces
Fix the wrinkles and smooth the creases.
But these tales are no longer in tatters
And now your review is all that matters.

If the London sky were a bit bluer
And the black clouds a bit fewer
If tropical skies were a bit duller
And London skies a different colour

And if Tower Bridge were a pinball flipper
And the London Eye would spin quicker.
If City Hall hadn't been built
At that funny tilt.

And if the Thames didn't twist and snake
As if there'd been a sudden earthquake.
Then London wouldn't be as it is
And we wouldn't know where we is.

But with black taxis and minicabs
Yellow lines and paving slabs.
Red pillar boxes and Postman Pat
We know where we are when we see all that.

At Lords a ball bounced towards the wicket
A batsman thought he couldn't miss it.
He had a few swings and a swipe for luck
But he was out for a duck.

An allrounder had a few tries
Now try this one on for size.
He knocked it for six over the fence
That happens a lot in these events.

Coming down from very high
Laws of Cricket would apply.
The ball without a sound
Bounced back in the ground.

A fielder gave a shout
Owzat! and caught him out.
The umpire wasn't very sure
But in or out the law's the law.

The Ponytails headed towards
The wax museum of Madam Tussauds.
And the quickest way to all things waxy
Was in the back of a black taxi.

The cabbie was Taxi Jack
I've 'ad 'em all in the back.
But Jack was already leaving our tale
His taxicab was up for sale.

This cab's yours for a monkey
It's a runner just a bit clunky.
A monkey was a bargain
That's £500 quid in London jargon.

The Ponytails were soon among famous people
From Henry VIII to a Beatle.
After dark they might start to talk
Move about and ball of chalk.

Henry VIII was jousting in the palace grounds
With ons and offs and ups and downs.
Unseated, unsaddled, dived
Thrown, befuddled, survived.

Shakespeare was posing with his wife
Inky quill and penknife.
Blots, stains and smudges
Piled high among the plots and grudges.

Harry Potter couldn't tell
If he was made of wax or a spell.
Had he been turned into this bad boy
By Voldemort or Malfoy?

Dick Whittington and his cat
The Pied Piper and a rat.
Dick Turpin and his horse
Maid Marion and Robin, of course.

Maid Marian and Robin Hood
Were hiding in Sherwood.
Little John was counting to ten
Then started searching with the merry men.

Bond, James Bond
Was called 007 by a blond.
When we're alone call me Jim
They broke the mould when they made him.

Ringo Starr was looking groovy
Love and peace and funky jewellery.
There's something about this drummer
Attracts us like no other.

Madame Tussaud's was just the place
To see what's her name or what's his face.
Every model polished and buffed
So much better than being stuffed.

The Cutty Sark full of Rosie Lee
Came back across the high sea.
Tossed and turned left to right
Like a Ponytail in a pillow fight.

At seven bells tea was drunk
In swinging hammock or lumpy bunk.
On every voyage short or long
The skipper had the kettle on.

The Cutty Sark was like a tea chest
Filled to the brim from hold to crow's nest.
Just the place when a storm was brewing
To have a cuppa in the rigging.

Anchors away and under sail
The kettle was on never fail.
Everyone stirring and sipping together
Through doldrums, squalls and bad weather.

There's a little teashop on the Greenwich Road
Where Hanoverian kings in days of old.
Had their tea by the pot
Saying chin! chin! and what! what! a lot.

Now, a brief word for the dunking fan
Always start with a plan.
When you're ready to take the plunge
Have a dip but never lunge.

As we thought and as expected
London's where this art was perfected.
As we can now clearly see
It all began with high tea.

At around eleven when they felt the urge
Nothing could stop the elevenses splurge.
Fairies, Eccles and tarts in hand
And fancies piled high on every cake stand.

And before portion control made a whinger
Out of many a café binger.
It was five spoons of sugar or lump it
And lots of butter on your crumpet.

With sponges, scones and apple pie
Scones, buns and pies piled high.
Someone must have taken that first dunk
Before the tea or coffee got drunk.

There's no plaque to mark the spot
Speculation's all we've got.
There's no one to take the credit
But someone must've done it.

With the coffee so piping hot
And the tea steaming in the pot.
There's one more thing you should know
Never suck when you should blow.

An escapologist named Keyhole Karl
Was the slowest lock picker by a mile.
Rolling around on the ground
With arms and legs shackled and bound.

Keyhole knew cos he'd been told
First things first and take off the blindfold.
But in the dark sack
Keyhole was losing track.

Where to begin?
Was it one pin for getting in
Or two for getting out?
Keyhole was losing count.

And was that a tickle between his toes
Or a spider up his nose?
If only the sack were a bit wider
To make more room for the spider.

A pride of Lions in Trafalgar Square
Liked to see more Ponytails there.
The lions guarded their water hole
And never moved what self-control.

And above in weather foul or fair
Nelson kept the wind from his hair.
A big hat kept it back and flat
Not everyone would've thought of that.

Lord Nelson or Horatio to his barber
Would have his hair cut in the harbour.
Horatio or Horace if you knew him better
Was a haircutting trend setter.

Admiral Nelson now looks down reminiscing
Comb hand on his sword and mirror hand missing.
But have a closer look and you won't fail
To see the Admiral's ponytail.

Catherine gazed in a fountain of water
A little closer than she ought a.
Her reflection drifted between lions' paws
Ever closer to their jaws.

The lions yawned and licked their lips
Catherine hung on by her fingertips.
Would the lions pounce and bite?
Could Catherine put up a fight?

She would make a tasty snack
The lions were about to attack.
Would her bones break and crunch?
Were the lions ready to munch?

Or she could be swallowed in one go
If nothing were done to stop the flow?
Not to worry a London chap
Put his hand in and turned off the tap.

As the rain fell on Shaftesbury Avenue
Catherine tripped and lost a shoe.
It's not the first time she's had to hop
Between lost shoe and soggy sock.

It was Catherine's usual trouble
Hoping from puddle to puddle.
Blown inside out by her umbrella
Oh! poor Cinderella.

Dr. Watson considered this a serious matter
And invited the Ponytails in for a natter.
But would Sherlock have a clue
How to find Catherine's shoe?

Could this be down to Moriarty?
Would they need a search party?
But no this had happened in other places
It could only be caused by snappy laces.

In Buckingham Palace there was a chauffeur
Who drove a car he called Motor.
In the stables there was a groom
Who kept a horse he called Boom.

The palace was just the place
For a Motor v Boom race.
Perhaps the groom should've made it clear
He didn't think this was a good idea.

The starting line was drawn
With tyre tracks across the lawn.
The finishing line was the main driveway
What would the owners say?

Before Boom joined the army
He was entered in the Epsom Derby.
But champion racer or show jumper
He wasn't getting any younger.

Motor too had seen better days
He once raced at Brands Hatch or so he says.
But bumper to bumper sump and pump
Nothing could make Motor jump.

Boom was doing his best
What happened next no one guessed.
A slide and skid are all it takes
To crash through the palace gates.

Wheels were losing their grip
Horseshoes were starting to slip.
But Boom was in luck
Motor was getting stuck.

Out on the Mall they went faster and faster
If they hadn't stopped it could've been a disaster.
Rumbling and thundering around Piccadilly
But could a horse really beat a car? don't be silly!

In Buckingham Palace there's a carriage
That's not only for weddings and marriage.
Whenever a royal needs to pop out
It's used as a regal runabout.

It's just the job for popping
Round the corner for the shopping.
Or they can take a shortcut
Through the park when it's shut.

Of course, you're not allowed to approach
This ceremonial state stagecoach.
But if you did try to hitch hike
They can stop for you if they like.

It would be good to ride
With a picnic deep inside.
Fizzy drinks and cream cakes
Bouncing over London's cobbles and shakes.

The Ponytails saw a man with spray paint
Decorating walls in Billingsgate.
If it were a fish, a balloon or just a splatter
Really didn't matter.

Without going into details
Banksy painted the Ponytails.
A tasteful portrait in brush and stencil
And finished off in pen and pencil.

Graffiti is forgivable
If it's a Banksy original.
Was it at Bank or the Stock Market
Where the rules were swept under the carpet?

A rainbow spanned from Roman Wall
Over Tower Bridge and City Hall.
On top were Ponytails and a painter
Riding the rainbow like an escalator.

You never know who you might meet
Walking down Downing Street.
Larry the mouser was on patrol
In plain clothes and on the payroll.

Palmerston nipped down the backstairs
Taking a break from foreign affairs.
Things could get a little stuffy
When your fur is long and fluffy.

Side by side they walked the beat
Up and down Downing Street.
But Larry could get very snooty
About always being first on duty.

Let me go first I know the way
Oh! that's what you always say.
Larry had made his point
He was top cat in this joint.

A sparrow flew from Big Ben
Over Whitehall to Number Ten.
Let me in from the rain
And I won't trouble you again.

Just a little birdseed
Is all I will need.
And a place to preen my feathers
I'm a sparrow of simple pleasures.

The Prime Minister appeared in the window
And said my shiny black door is just below.
And I think if it's all up to me
You're as welcome as a birdie can be.

The sparrow flew to the table to hop, pick and peck
That's what puts the bounce in a birdie's step.
I know that means thank you in your chirpy ways
There's no need for thank yous or your chirpy praise.

Time to say goodnight
And start the Ponytail pillow fight.
But should we reconsider our position
And put an end to this tradition?

Some say pillow fights ain't proper
Stop before they have to stop yer.
That's just like health and safety
But let's not be too hasty.

Let loose a driving skew-whiffer
With best regards from a well-wisher.
Head over feathers in rough and tumble
Walloped and wobbled in a bouncing jumble.

Decked, wrecked and clouted in a moment of doubt
Pummelled, rattled and turned inside out.
If you're rebounded, befuddled in a pillow burst
Always remember, safety first.

And now a sort of epilogue
To complete this Ponytail travelogue.
As the Boden Hall clock chimes through the night
They picked up the feathers and turned out the light.

After getting home from their globetrot
The Ponytails settle down to swot.
But all work and no play
Was never the Ponytails' way.

As night fell over Boden Hall
There was not a sound, nothing at all.
It was quiet then but just a mo
With Ponytails you never know.

Time enough to reminisce
And remember London with their favourite Miss.
Soon plans would be laid
For a brand-new escapade.

End

Rome

This Ponytail Tale was found far from home
In an old *caffè* in the centre of Rome.
Left in haste by an unsettled bill
Exactly where's a mystery still.

These pages were found jumbled and rumpled
Unwanted, creased and crumpled.
Then experts with ink and glue
Put them together as good as new.

It may have been all go and pressure
With sticky fingers stuck together.
Inky spots and inky spurts
Running down inky shirts.

It wasn't easy to unjumble the bits and pieces
Fix the wrinkles and smooth the creases.
But these tales are no longer in tatters
And now your review is all that matters.

In the *Piazza di Spagna*, a boat was scuppered
How the crew must've gurgled and spluttered.
Was the captain the last to abandon ship
And hold his nose for a choppy dip?

The Ponytails wanted to see more
And get closer and closer to explore.
They peeped through a splintered crack
And saw the same faces peeping back.

The Ponytails' reflection was very wet
Pouring and spilling out a drippy outlet.
Who could change the leak's direction
And rescue the Ponytails' reflection?

There were no lifeguards about
They had nobody to pull them out.
Then as quickly as it had begun
The clouds blotted out the sun.

What caused this mishap?
Did the anchor slip and the mainsail snap?
Could it have been a weather forecaster
Who got it wrong and caused a disaster?

Did the timbers squeak and creek
Before springing that fatal leak?
Did the navigator lose the plot
To wash up on this unlikely spot?

To find out there's no need to go far
We know where the crew now are.
The crew soon got a grip
And were quick to abandon the leaky ship.

Luigi was the *capitano*
Who bought the *Caffè Buon Giorno.*
Now a local celebrity
Luigi's never going back to sea.

The Ponytails had the idea
To have lunch in a *pizzeria*.
No-one flips dough like a *pizza* man
Like tossing pancakes without the pan.

The Ponytails put on a show
Throwing and twirling the *pizza* dough.
Knuckles kneaded for a sling
Then throwing the mix for a high fling.

Once flung and given a spin
They opened the oven and bunged it in.
A whopping 240 degrees for the extra topping
That's a lot of slicing and chopping.

Just one pizza if it's a biggy
Could feed the whole Roman city.
This may appear farfetched
But it could even feed more at a stretch.

On the *Via Giulia* Catherine tripped and lost a shoe
What made her slip she never knew.
It could've been some slippery two for one offer
Dropped by a careless *panino* scoffer.

What caused the Ponytail to stumble
And bounce downstairs in a tumble?
It wasn't her laces that made her scramble
Cos Catherine lost a sandal.

Toppled and wobbled, rumpled and crumpled
Head over heels the Ponytail tumbled.
Landing tangled in the *centro* di *Roma*
Oh! poor *Cenerentola*.

It was so unfair
For Catherine to lose her footwear.
If only she could ride a *Lambretta* sideways on the back
With a bouquet of flowers on her lap.

In the *Caffè* Nero's Violin
Lived the furriest cat there's ever been.
Cleopatra was lying on the counter
Curlers and brushes all about 'er.

Her long tail hanging with a curl
On her diamond collar a silver bell.
Purring and rolling on her squeaky toys
Pawing and making a squeaky noise.

For any daring mice
Cleo had a word of sound advice.
Just a word in your ear
I'm not as soft as I may appear.

I see you mouse on my floor
If I get up you'll get what for.
Yea, you and who's army?
You big hairy salami.

Miss Balard was wrestling with a bottle of pop
Struggling and unable to unscrew the top.
Something wasn't right
The top was on too tight.

The top was a tight fit
Miss Balard couldn't unscrew it.
She took hold and let her thumb oppose
So, the bubbles wouldn't go up her nose.

Her usual squeeze and twist wouldn't do
Till there was a Ponytail breakthrough.
The Ponytails discovered the knack
To avoid this bother they took it back.

The Ponytails were plainspoken
Scusi Signore, this bottle won't open.
Grazie mille, now be a good man
And change this bottle for a can.

In the *Piazza Navona* a cephalopod
Was in competition with a Roman god.
An octopus rarely strays from his reef
To do battle in Rome, so that's a relief.

But Neptune was caught by a tentacle
And seven more similarly identical.
Why was Neptune gripped in this twist and throttle?
Where was *Polpo* when we couldn't open the bottle?

No explanation would be needed
If the octopus succeeded.
But after so many historical conflicts
Neptune knew all his eight-legged tricks.

Nine brains, eight legs and thrice hearted
An octopus can still be outsmarted.
After all his thrashing and bashing
Octopus was disqualified for splashing.

Dunking biscuits in Rome
Is much the same as back home.
Biscotto, biscotti or digestive dipper
Like having tea with the vicar.

Italians will be reclined
And as a rule are inclined
To have their *merenda* in a cup
And rarely dunk standing up.

We might think a Jammie Dodger or HobNob
Would do nicely and be just the job.
But the *l'inzuppare* or dunking devotee
Will always favour the *biscotti*.

And there's one thing you might find
The Romans are very refined.
Because no matter how long a soggy bit lingers
They'll never get it out with their fingers.

With a swagger a snigger and a snarl
Came the escapologist Keyhole Karl.
Come on Carlo it's not a trick
You can pick the lock and get out quick.

Avanti Carlo and the best of luck
Mind your head and don't forget to duck.
It only takes a nudge to open the top
A jiggle a wriggle and out you pop.

It may just be tittle-tattle
Or silly talk that'll
Make you wonder if the truth be told
Was Keyhole really so bold?

But what if squashed and restricted
I bump my bonce as predicted.
Not to worry give us a shout
We'll tip you up and slide you out.

The Ponytails' good deed for the day
Was to help a cleric find his way.
After strolling along the *Via Appia*
He couldn't have been any happier.

Olive trees, lemons and limes
Shading brambles, quince and vines.
Ivy climbing peaches, pears and cherries
Apricots, damsons and red berries.

On this long and dusty trail
He was surprised to find a Ponytail.
Do you *parli Italiano*?
I can't find the *Vaticano*.

But in such a scene so *tutti frutti*
Could a Ponytail really find the way? absolutely.
Capisco Padre in not too many metres
You'll be back in Saint Peter's.

In the *Circus Maximus* a gladiator
Had a word with a spectator.
I've got a feeling and I can tell
Today won't end very well.

You came you saw you pondered
But have you ever wondered
Veni vidi vici
Why is Caesar's toga so itchy?

It's not easy being a gladiator
I was once Caesar's head waiter.
He used to eat with the troops
All camaraderie and spaghetti hoops.

I thought he was alright
Just not very bright.
But I just put my thumb in the boss' soup
And he called me a nincompoop.

Before I go, I want to confess
What I did to Caesar's dress.
When he was shouting louder and louder
I sprinkled him with itching powder.

And because Caesar is so unfair
I hid a whoopee cushion on his chair.
He said he'd clap me in irons
And now he wants me to feed the lions.

I was the one who got the admiring glances
Now I suppose I've spoilt my chances.
I'm a bit concerned I hope it's not showing
Let me know if there's any jobs going.

It's not nice to be chased in the arena.
Here he comes all hail Caesar!
I'm not afraid of that big pudding
I'll get him back when he's not looking.

When Caesar couldn't sleep
He counted the heads of sheep.
Or he counted the ears and divided by two
Like the Greeks used to do.

In a different time and age
Caesar let beasts out the cage.
A gladiator's worst nightmare
Was to be chased by a lion or a bear.

You can't reason with a lion there's no debate
You just have to run faster than your mate.
The lions took out their claws
Smacked their lips and wiggled their jaws.

Caesar could get very bored
But perked up when the lions roared.
Faster puss catch that one
He put a whoopee cushion under my bum.

A homeless *sanztetto* in evening dress
Gave the *Parco del Celio* as his address.
On the bench where he sat
Slept his pal his hairy cat.

A flock of parakeets lived there too
Just a few at first but the flock grew.
Bene, bene now there are so many
But before there weren't any.

The Ponytails held out their hands full of seed
So, the little birds would come and feed.
And they came by the score
Plus, dozens and dozens and dozens more.

What clatter came out those beaks
What chatter and strange shrieks.
Here there's room for everyone
Said the *sanztetto* and his chum.

A little girl in a green dress and red hairband
Gripped a note and coins in her hand.
She was trying to get home to her mum
But which way had she come?

She couldn't remember her way home
Among the *stradas* and *vias* of Rome.
It's so easy to get lost
When *vicolos* and *piazzas* have been crossed.

The little girl was in distress
Dropped a bottle of milk and made a mess.
An *agente di polizia* ran over on the double
The *ragazzina* was crying was she in trouble?

Calmati said our cop
I'll pop back to the shop.
And so he did in a hurry
So, there was no need to worry.

Across the Roman skyline
Bells ring out from time to time.
But little birds are seldom prepared
And fly off scattered and scared.

Bigger birds as a rule
Stay put and try to look cool.
A stork flew in for a rest
Met his mate and built a nest.

Here we are my dear will this do?
Have a perch and admire the view.
But look over there my lanky beaky squawker
Can't you see the aqueduct has running water?

That's alright my sweet wading duck
It's only a pile of sticks and muck.
If only I had a bit more warning
I'll shift it first thing in the morning.

A *supermercato* trolley rattling and wobbly
Could look a bit like a roman chariot, most probably.
A good run up by the Ponytail forces
Could make up for any lack of horses.

Rolling from place to place
The Ponytails had a chariot race.
A red Ferrari cruising past
Wasn't nearly half as fast.

Painted red to make it go faster
The Ferrari was trying to get past her.
If the Ponytails were charioteers
They'd beat a Ferrari or so it appears.

The chequered flag was getting near
The winner was still unclear.
But could a supermarket trolly all wobbly and tinny
Really go faster than a Ferrari? don't be silly.

When Rome's night sky is deepest black
Showing signs of the zodiac.
Romans wish on distant stars
And Jupiter aligns with Mars.

Where gods may argue and bicker
Is that a Plough or a Big Dipper?
And if you join up the dots
Are they jugs or water pots?

Is fate decided by the gods
Pointing us out with winks and nods?
Are they looking down from Rome's night sky
From Aries, Taurus and Gemini?

Might the gods set you an epic quest
To slay a dragon or pass some test?
And then turn you into a donkey or bunny
I suppose they think that's funny.

I know what you're thinking and you're right
It's time for a Ponytail pillow fight.
All's fair in such times as these
There's no need for referees.

Gladiators too would start the night
With a no holds barred pillow fight.
Funny enough and as luck would have it
The Ponytails were of the same habit.

It all started for some reason
When Caesar challenged an entire legion.
All those boffs and grunts
But Caesar was never hit once.

When in Rome do as the Romans do
There's nothing to fear until one hits you.
Once again the feathers were flying
Swerve and duck there's no harm trying.

And now a sort of epilogue
To complete this Ponytail travelogue.
As the Boden Hall clock chimed through the night
They picked up the feathers and turned out the light.

As night fell over Boden Hall
There was not a sound nothing at all.
It was quiet then but just a mo
With Ponytails you never know.

After arriving home from their globetrot
The Ponytails settle down to swot.
But all work and no play
Was never the Ponytails' way.

Time enough to reminisce
And remember Rome with their favourite Miss.
Soon plans would be laid
For a brand-new escapade.

Barcelona

This Ponytail Tale was found in Spain
In the dining car of a RENFE train.
Left in haste by an unsettled bill
Exactly where's a mystery still.

It may have been all go and pressure
With sticky fingers stuck together.
And inky spots and inky spurts
Running down inky shirts.

Rearranging papers, doodles and scribbles
Jottings, scrawls and squiggles.
Piecing together notes and scraps
And filling in holes and gaps, perhaps.

It wasn't easy to unjumble the bits and pieces
Fix the wrinkles and smooth the creases.
But these tales are no longer in tatters
And now your review is all that matters.

A waiter had the longest moustache ever
It was well kept and trained, however.
Starched and waxed by the *camarero*
With room to perch a chirpy sparrow.

The birds they are my friends
They come and go it just depends.
Once I had six on this side
My moustache is long my moustache is wide.

They like to sit in rows
And build a nest up my nose.
They are very skilled
Look how my nose is filled.

If I blow my nose I mustn't squeeze
They're not 'appy when I sneeze.
But the nest it prickle
I sneeze a lot when it tickle.

A *Chico* with his sweet tootsie
Looked nervous playing footsie.
With fate tempted and a coin tossed
The *Chico* had his fingers crossed.

The young man had a suggestion
On bended knee he popped the question.
Full of hope and ring extended
He awaited the answer of his intended.

He was twitching and biting his nails
Looked on by the Ponytails.
He offered her a solitaire in a gypsy claw
Could his tootsie ask for more?

Would his diamond ring impress?
Would his lovely tootsie say yes?
But she was quick to decide
Sí, sí, sí she replied.

A bullfighter was very busy
Fighting a bull in a tizzy.
It's not easy doing battle
With touchy Spanish cattle.

The bull turned so sharply
It caught the torero's tights so sparkly.
Oh, no! Not another ladder
The bull was getting madder and madder.

¡Olé! with a swivel and a swerve
A *matador* must keep his nerve.
Risking everything on a toss
Heads, tails, a win or loss.

A *Picador* took a gamble
And got his spurs in a tangle.
Bareback without a saddle
Up the creek without a paddle.

With a mop of curly hair
And hands in pockets without a care
A *chico* gave a cheeky whistle
Thinking this'll

Help to lighten the mood
With a musical interlude.
¡Música! ¡Música! the crowd requested
And a catchy tune was suggested.

The *chico* came with the intention
Of demonstrating his latest invention.
A tuba you play with elbows or knees.
Or handsfree if there's a breeze.

It's bound to be the latest craze
The next thing and all the rage.
Everyone will want one of these
You don't blow you just squeeze.

Along the Ramblas raced a horse and carriage
With a bride and groom and their baggage.
By their side but even faster
Came another courting disaster.

A third was closing on the rails
Thundering past the Ponytails.
Bridesmaids and their posies
Petunias, Margaritas and Roses.

Coming up behind a coach and four
There wasn't room for anymore.
Out the way! Coming through!
What d'yer think we're trying to do?

Came a *Guardia Civil* on his horse
He had the law to enforce.
Two in hand or a coach and four
Fast or slow the law's the law.

Gargoyles have hung out in the *Barrio Gótico*,
In that district so old and *histórico*,
Since those first kings of Spain's
Built the cathedrals and the drains.

In the drain lived a fly called Mosca
Who had a girlfriend until he lost 'er.
When the gargoyle overflowed
And washed his precious down the road.

Life gives and life undoes
How he would miss her hum and buzz.
Never again would he see her evade some rotter
With a rolled-up newspaper or fly swatter.

How graceful was her swerve and spin
But it wasn't a game she could always win.
His love was now for ever plighted
Until the day they'd be reunited.

In the *Plaza Real* a stamp collection
Had a stamp with an imperfection.
The queen's head was upside down
And wearing a hat instead of a crown.

But it wasn't the queen it was her brother
The prince of somewhere or other.
Fair's fair and rules are rules
He's not allowed to wear crown jewels.

Her majesty can't be an imposter
Where's the queen? I think we've lost her.
Fair's fair and a joke's a joke
Her majesty can't be a bloke.

In a big value starter pack
Queens were shaken from front to back.
Crowned heads lost control
Heads were knocked and heads would roll.

A skinny cyclist in baggy shorts
Cycled up Tibidabo, it takes all sorts.
With his head down by the bell
And rear up high he was doing well.

Nearing the top, he was getting weaker
But nothing would stop this thrill seeker.
He wouldn't give up at any cost.
With pedals whirling all was not lost.

The cyclist clung to just one hope
To not come off the steepest slope.
He couldn't give in till he'd done it
Onwards and upwards to the summit.

At the top on his bike so trusty
He opened a map when it was gusty.
The map took off in the air
And it was all downhill from there.

Dressed in blue and red
And bouncing a football on her head.
Came a *nena fútbolista*
And doing keepie-uppies came her sister.

The *Barça Señoritas'* team
Are tougher than they seem.
The *futbolistas* kicked the ball
And the Ponytails kicked an' all.

Only three goals to decide the winner
Cos they had to shoot off for dinner.
The Ponytails knew for sure
The best of three can't be a draw.

Three's a win and one's a loss
And two's what they call *dos*.
If lunch and time permits
They'd score one each and call it quits.

The Ponytails went perchance
To a Catalan *Sardana* dance.
In circles holding hands
Danced the dancing Catalans.

The Ponytails liked a lot
Dancing slowly on the spot.
There're only two steps short and long
Nice and slow what could go wrong?

The *Castellers* put a girl on top
Who began to slip, slide and drop.
When a lost map blew from some place
Around the tower and in her face.

The human tower began to wilt
Waddle, totter and tilt.
The tower fell like a giant banana
Across the Ponytails' *sardana.*

In Barcelona roots and shoots began to appear
But what they were made of wasn't clear.
Were they made of vegetation.
Or someone's imagination?

An architect thought he knew
How to build a church as if it grew.
And he built it so well
If it grew or not you couldn't tell.

Could a church grow out the ground
Like a vine climbing round and round?
With its roots, buds and shoots
Sprouting columns, vaults and fruits?

Did nature really take a back seat
To the pouring of cement and concrete?
Were foundations ever needed
Or was this plot hoed and seeded?

Between arrival and departure
There's always time for *horchata*.
The waiter recommended
The *horchata* smooth and blended.

Never gunky or globular
Horchata's always been popular.
And you get a white moustache
If you drink out the glass.

Leave the straw and drink up
Out the glass or out the cup.
Stick a finger in and give it a lick
Horchata or chocolate take your pick.

According to insiders
Horchata is much loved by tigers.
As you'd soon see
If you ever had a tiger to tea.

If Picasso, Miró and Dalí could meet
In a *café* on some street.
And doodle on a tablecloth
To pay the bill or get a bit off.

Or frequent some other venue
And draw little fish on the menu.
Birds or fish in a shoal
In pen and ink or charcoal.

Then they could pay to go out to dine
Just on a little squiggly line.
Because you never know what a sketch
Original and signed could fetch.

Just a squiggle or a scrawl
Could find its way on the wall.
It could be worth a lot you might find
If it's drawn by the undersigned.

In the *Plaza de España* a photographer chappie
Was busy taking snap after snappie.
Clicks and pics nonstop
Flash, dazzle and crop.

Portrait or landscape
Every picture was in good shape.
Adjusting shutters for wideness and brightness
This cameraman took a good likeness.

Saying watch the birdie and say cheese
There were no limits to his expertise.
He might've zoomed out instead of in
And his closeups weren't what they should've been.

He might forget to remove the lens cover
Or open some speeding shutter or other.
But he always took a good mugshot
And did his best with what he's got.

On the *Montjuïc* mountain
The Ponytails found a fountain.
And lay on the edge where it's cool and shady
Fishy tales and Ponytails all mermaidy.

Will Catherine's reflection be calm and still
Or will something happen? of course it will.
It shot up in a jet of water
The Ponytails should have caught 'er.

But they used the wrong technique
Grabby pouncy, so to speak.
The Ponytails grab and pounce
Couldn't stop Catherine's bounce.

It should've been their greatest catch
But it was another grab and snatch.
The Ponytails got in a muddle
And Catherine dropped in a puddle.

Barcelona has created
Many ways to keep Ponytails hydrated.
There's not only Fantas and *horchatas*
There's *gazpacho andaluz* too for starters.

Gazpacho cold and chilled
Diced, chopped and peeled.
Who could've predicted
Salad works as a liquid?

Chocolate and *churros* we might suppose
Could make a mess of your clothes.
But highly trained in their tuck shop
The Ponytails never spilt a drop.

An *ensaimada* with angel's hair
Was left untouched and going spare.
Because dunking such a large confection
Was completely out of the question.

With just a little language in this country
You would never go thirsty or hungry.
Ask for *el menú*
And see if you know what to do.

You can get *ensalada, tomate, patatas and vinagre*
Hamburguesa, fruta, melón and *chocolate.*
Oh! You didn't know you know
So much *español.*

Just a little or *una mica*
Is enough to be a speaker.
Oh! You didn't know you can
Speak a little Catalan.

Ponytails learn languages at school.
It's what they like best as a rule.
But get away as quick as they can
To see for themselves, that's the plan.

It was where Columbus looks out to sea
Remembering when only he
Had the knack
To find America and his way back

That Miss Balard was swept along
With the, He's a *Muchacho Excelente* song.
But clapping and singing in the midsection
The Ponytails were straying in the wrong direction.

Turistas on the corner
Jumped to their feet and tried to warn 'er.
But *the Ramblas* were much too crowded
And no-one heard a word they shouted.

Would the Ponytails be lost in the far reaches
Or marooned on distant beaches?
No back they came safe and sound
That's because the world is round.

It has never really come to light
Why Ponytails pillow fight.
But it's one in the eye for the mollycoddled
When they are boffed and nobbled.

Pillows make the best gobstopper
If you're gonna bop 'em proper.
Rock 'em back on their heels
off their feet in twirls and swirls.

Last one standing in a pillow fight
Makes the bed and turns out the light.
It's a time for simple pleasures
Fix your hair and pick up the feathers.

Ponytails have the knack
To biff and boff front and back.
Straightened doubled and bended
Is often the way these tales ended.

And now a sort of epilogue
To complete this Ponytail travelogue.
As the Boden Hall clock chimed through the night
The Ponytails slept tighty-tight.

As night fell over Boden Hall
There was not a sound nothing at all.
It was quiet then but just a mo
With Ponytails you never know.

Back home from their globetrot
The Ponytails settled down to swot.
But all work and no play
Was never the Ponytails' way.

Time enough to reminisce
And remember Barcelona with their favourite Miss.
Soon plans would be laid
For a brand-new escapade.

Fin

Brussels

This Ponytail Tale was found in Belgium
Where such tales turn up seldom.
Left in haste by an unsettled bill
Exactly where is a mystery still.

These pages were found damp and curly
But lucky enough they caught it early.
It must have taken the experts ages
To dry these papers and soggy pages.

Helped by modern science
And a hair drying appliance.
Scientific advances and the hairdryer
Donated by a local supplier

Everyone knew when they started
This was no job for the faint hearted.
But they knew your review would be glowing
And that's what kept 'em going.

A little boy wasn't meant to be
On the *Rue de l'Etuve* having a wee.
But now he'd started he couldn't stop
It was getting deeper by the drop.

Up an alley tucked away
In the *Impasse de la Fidélité*.
A little girl was having a tinkle
Giving the rocks and plants a sprinkle.

On *Chartreux* street not far away
On that very same day.
A dog went up a post
Where he liked to go the most.

Then a road sweeper made a swap
Swapping his broom for a mop.
And now we know the reason why
It's so hard to keep Brussels dry.

Speaking of Brussels statues
There are *beaucoup* to choose.
From *art nouveau*
To *Madame Chapeau.*

A work in stone or it could be granite
Was chiselled and hammered with a mallet.
Now the Soldier-Pigeons are remembered
Never a one ever surrendered.

A copper on *Molenbeek* patrol
Was tripped up and lost control.
Grabbed by the ankle what a pity
That's no way to treat the *politie.*

By *Saint Nicolas* church you might find
The blind leading the blind.
Holding on to just one stick
That's their usual trick.

René Magritte was painting doggies
Cats in hats and raining moggies.
But did he paint by day or night
When the day was dark and the night was light?

Could bright clouds mean rain
Or was he up to his old tricks again?
Bowlers and brollies you wouldn't forget
Were falling from the sky over Jette.

A pipe was puffing smoke
That's not a pipe. Sorry I spoke.
But that is a train coming out the chimney
I'll get on quick if you don't believe me.

However sunny or dark the street
You can still tell it's Magritte.
Like with his ear on or off
You can still tell it's Van Gogh.

A Tintin story often begins
With help from the Thompson twins.
Thomson and Thompson were drawn together
Solving mysteries with the Professor.

Snowy has a nose for a scoop
He's one of the gang and in the loop.
He'd sniff out the news he's very sniffy
Clear up the mess in a jiffy.

Hold the front page and stop the presses
Another Tintin plot progresses.
To cut a short story shorter
Tintin's Brussels' ace reporter.

Captain Haddock might get confused
Bewildered, baffled and bemused.
But he does his best. Blistering barnacles!
Let him stick that in his articles.

Never leave the lower town for the upper
Before grabbing a quick cuppa.
Hopping in the street elevator
Saying see you later alligator.

Yes, it's best to have a cuppa
Before taking the lift up to the upper.
Never do it the other way round
Cos there's no *café* on the higher ground.

And in Brussels you dunk a *Speculoo*
It would be rude not to.
Never ever a Belgian bun
Cos they ain't got none.

And remember while you're up town
What goes up must come down.
The lift's the best way to go
From *Palais de Justice* to Marolles.

Following a recent success
Poirot arrived on the Orient Express.
It was a twisty turney plot
But Poirot knew whodunit or not.

The Ponytails are *demoiselles*
And also have little grey cells.
Hercule Poirot said as much
He had a way with words and such.

Praise from Poirot is praise indeed
All the praise a Ponytail needs.
That's what makes it all worthwhile
Brussels tonight tomorrow the Nile.

When all's said and done
Poirot's the best under the sun.
He makes it look as easy as ABC
N'est-ce pas, mon amie?

L'Ultime Atome was the place
In the *Rue Saint-Boniface*
Where the Ponytails were awash
With fancy-schmancy Belgian nosh.

Where to start?
Plat du jour or *à la carte*?
Mussels and chips and mayonnaise
Oh! happy days.

A place to spend their pocket-money
On waffles and ice-cream cos it's sunny.
Strawberries and cream piled high
For the Ponytails to try.

But just how yummy are Brussels sprouts?
The Ponytails had their doubts.
Do all good things come in little packages
Even tiny wannabe cabbages?

On the *Place du Jeu de balle*
The Ponytails were on the trail
Of a valued antique
Very rare and unique.

Collectibles and curios
Where they're from no-one knows.
Perhaps an eighteenth-century survivor
A snip for just under a fiver.

They found two vases by *Val Saint Lambert*
In need of repair.
But with a splidgy splodgy gel
They were fixed up so you can't tell.

In the *Marché aux Puces* you might find a trinket
A bauble or a bagatelle don't over think it.
Then the *Café Volle Brol* is the ideal haunt
For Ponytails to look at what they've bought.

If the *Atomium's* nine balls or spheres
Came apart it'd end in tears.
Like a snooker break
One tap is all it takes.

Or could they drop off one day
Bounce about and roll away?
Which one would bounce the highest
The heaviest one or the lightest?

What if they rattled around *Laeken*
Chased by dogs barking and shaken?
Sharp teeth and wagging tails
Snappy snips, woofs and growls.

What if the Ponytails gave chase
And it turned into a race?
Trips, pushes and pulls
Ponytails, dogs and balls.

The river Senne sounds the same
As Paris' River *Seine*.
Today it's not so easily found
Since it went underground.

But Catherine could see in *Saint-Géry*
How the *Senne* used to be.
The coolest place on a sunny day
To watch her reflection drift away.

A kingfisher fell out the sky
Dearie me I wonder why?
Plopping down in the *Senne*
Bringing Catherine back again.

Perhaps Catherine never regretted
Getting her reflection soaked and wetted.
A visage not to forget
Sun dried or dripping wet.

The Ponytails hopped on tram 44
Montgomery to Tervuren door to door.
Tervuren and the *Mussé du Congo*
Lolloping like a rocking bongo.

Rattling along to see the exhibits
No queuing cos they had tickets.
Leopard, eland and okapi
Some had spots and some were stripy.

A wildebeest or a gnu
Was looking about having a chew.
Asking everyone what's your name?
But he didn't have one. What a shame.

The Bandundu Water Jazz Band
Was tuning up on the fountain stand.
Saying, why not walk in the spray
On such a lovely Tervuren day.

In Grand Place the Town Hall's spire
Twists and leans climbing higher and higher.
And among its ins and outs and in-betweens
A little bat hangs out and dreams.

Dreams of a time long ago
When a market bustled down below.
Where so many things new and old
Were bartered, bought and sold.

Lace, damask and moquette
Exchanged hands in a *tête-à-tête*.
And sweet buns out the oven
Were sold still warm by the dozen.

Perhaps a chance to trade glances too
To meet new people you never knew.
Many dream of things like that
If you're a girl, boy or bat.

Straight, crinkly or curled
The best chips in the world
Start life in Belgium's mud
Just a poor simple spud.

Then lifted from the muddy field
Scrubbed up nicely and peeled.
And given the chance to leap
Into the oil, hot and deep.

And somewhere deep down in the heat
A chip and a *frite* collide and meet.
Somehow their destinies conspire
To bring them together in the frier.

Just the place for them to click
Teflon coated and non-stick.
Then a serving suggestion before they part
Mayo or ketchup? that's *à la carte*.

Wham! Bam! the cat Splash
Fell asleep in a flash.
Splash like cats of many colours
Could sleep in beds or even gutters.

Or on a doormat
If it came to that.
But Splash was more of a sofa king
That's really what worked for him.

Splash stuck to sofas like glue
Like an Indian in his igloo.
On the divan he was king
That's really what worked for him.

Splash had many dreams and nightmares
Snoozing on Brussels' divans and chairs.
Splash was the cat who would be king
That's really what worked for him.

Between the Royal Palace and *Bozar*
Where the underneaths and ruins are.
Jumps out a ghost nearly every night
Scaring people with a fright.

And his mate as white as a sheet
Does the same on *Hermosa* Street.
Some say they were dukes
Who lost their heads and now they're spooks.

And on *Amigo* Street a late grandee
Was once a bigwig in Burgundy.
Before he did something improper
Faced the block and the chopper.

High above hooting owls
Were looking down with hoots and scowls.
The Ponytails like all those
And passed by on tippy toes.

Between Parc and Merode
Near that very busy road.
The Ponytails wondered around two squares
The best ones always come in pairs.

In *Ambiorix* and *Marie Louise*
With fountains like becalmed seas.
And the distant hum of a lawn mower
Everything seemed slower and slower.

If the lawns were never mowed
And if the fountains overflowed
Could the Ponytails drift on green seas
From Ambiorix to *Marie Louise*?

With such thoughts and daydreams
Gazes and how it seemed.
The Ponytails were adrift in their stares
Wonderings and Brussels squares.

Skipping puddles in the rain
Catherine lost a shoe again.
It was gone in a bish bash bosh
Or was it a splish splash splosh?

Dunked like a *Speculoo*
Catherine lost another shoe.
She saw it go from her drippy umbrella
Oh! poor Cinderella.

But there's no time for sorrow
Chin up there's always tomorrow.
That's the Ponytail way
Tomorrow's another day.

Anyway, Miss Ballard was helpin'
Had a look and stuck her hand in.
And fished out the soggy shoe
Just like you would do.

The Ponytails had a theory
Why the Chunnel was so dreary.
It's cos you can't look out
And see what's swimming round about.

Let's have windows here and there
A telescope and a deck chair.
The idea isn't so nutty
With double glazing and lots of putty.

We could wave at fish to see who's fastest
Who came first and who came lastest.
And if the track were shorter on the other side
We could have a paddle at low tide.

And shouldn't there be some devices
To pop outside in a crisis?
And would it be too much to ask
To have a snorkel and a mask?

Now could the time be right
For a Ponytail pillow fight?
Pillows at dusk the Ponytails' way
Part bundle part ballet.

A flying pillow on the rise
Caught a Ponytail by surprise.
Two kilos of feathers couldn't miss 'er
Between the eyes and in the kisser.

Pounce, bounce and stumble
Hoping their defences crumble.
Then a thwack with a view to
A direct hit on the tutu.

A *pirouette* in a *pas de deux*
En pointe what could occur?
And a plié with a *grande jeté*
Come on punk make my day.

And now a sort of epilogue
To end this Ponytail travelogue.
As the Boden Hall clock chimed through the night
The Ponytails slept tighty tight.

As night fell over Boden Hall
There was not a sound nothing at all.
It was quiet then but just a mo
With Ponytails you never know.

After arriving home from their globetrot
The Ponytails settled down to swot.
But all work and no play
Was never the Ponytails' way.

Time enough to reminisce
And remember Brussels with their favourite Miss.
Soon plans would be laid
For a brand-new escapade.

Fin

Sydney

Although there are few details
This Ponytail Tale was found in New South Wales.
Left in haste by an unsettled bill
Exactly where's a mystery still.

These pages were found dry and wrinkly
Frail, brittle and crinkly.
But now thanks to the scientific process
They're as good as new, more or less.

It may have been all hard yakka
For chook feed not worth a cracker.
Clearing every smudge and smidge
Fair dinkum and ridgy didge.

Working flat out like a lizard drinking
They knew what you'd be thinking.
They knew your review would be overflowing
And that's what kept 'em going.

The Ponytails knew what might've happened
As Cook's anchor dropped and his sails slackened.
Perhaps the Captain's cabin boy
Stood on the deck calling, land ahoy!

Perhaps he jumped, yelped and spun
And with that Australia could've begun.
The Ponytails would've done the same
But they weren't there, what a shame.

The Ponytails imagined life on the Endeavour
Rounding the Horn in bad weather.
They would've held on tight to the mizzen
As Endeavour was tossed and risen.

Theirs would've been the only ship in Botany Bay
If only they could've seen what's there today.
The Ponytails could see quite clearly
What must've happened or very nearly.

An Aussie went walkabout
Not with the Ponytails but without.
And a billabong was the perfect place
To take off his hat and cover his face.

To the hum of a lone mozzie
Settled back our walkabout Aussie.
While unseen on a muddy pile
Ready to snap was a crocodile.

And sneaking behind a salty rock
Ready to spring was another crock.
And where there was once a creek
A third was having a stickybeak.

He was caught napping, or was he?
It's hard to tell with an Aussie.
A croc snaps but rarely hurries
The Aussie eased back, no worries.

There's A Corner On The Macintyre
In the shade or under fire.
For Shearing The Rams and Wood Splitters
And is no place for quitters.

Rams graze and rams get fatter
Sheep spook and sheep scatter.
Rams are sheared and rams stray
Sheep follow and make A Break Away.

Socks get worn and socks get knitted
Trees are felled and wood gets splitted.
A Bushman Knits His Socks
And keeps his sheep in mobs not flocks.

A Swagman Down On His Luck or stony broke
Can count on a mate or another bloke.
And he knows After The Rain
He'll be in The Sunny South Again.

An Aussie dropped a sanger
Off the top of the Coathanger.
And spat the dummy as it spun out of sight
It must've been a Vegemite.

And dropped another off the top
Onto the Ponytails, plop! plop! plop!
Miss Ballard said it's time for tucker
When an idea suddenly struck 'er.

What if we had a bite on the harbour bridge?
She'll be right ridgy didge.
The Ponytails had Tim Tams and Pavlova
For when the climb up there was over.

And without more ado
Stood back to admire the view.
And thought when it's really clear
You could see the new year from here.

A blowie and a joey had a race
Through shrub and scrub to another place.
Starting where a billy was a simmer
First one back would be the winner.

The Aussie salute got 'em going
Huffing, puffing and blowing.
Eat my dust! shouted the baby roo
No, you eat mine and hooroo.

Taking the lead raced the joey
Chased by the bzzzzing blowie.
The blowie was getting excited
The billy had been sighted.

First back to the billy where it had all begun
Was the blowie; the blowie won.
But would a blowie really be first back to the billy?
Don't be silly!

The Ponytails went walkabout
It's good to squiz and get out.
It was the Ponytails' lucky day
When the koalas came to play.

You never see very many
And sometimes there aren't any.
It's hard to see more than three
Up a eucalyptus tree.

Even a pair is quite rare
For the lonely koala bear.
Koalas are rarely seen in tens
They never have so many friends.

But the Ponytails saw plenty
A score or more or even twenty.
That's a lot for one outing
But who's counting?

The Opera House was obscured
Because of where a ship was moored.
Ships tie up and ships cruise
But shouldn't block Sydney's views.

It was docked and tied to the quay
The Ponytails were looking but couldn't see.
We're not ones to make a fuss
If it's no trouble, it's not just us.

Are you leaving at high tide?
We can't see the other side.
Or a bit more to the right would be good
Do you think you could?

You'd fit over there with a squeeze
Would you mind? Pretty please.
But with a face like a dropped pie
The captain turned making no reply.

Miss Ballard was surfing in sunnies and slouch hat
And a ring around her middle so's not to fall flat.
Legs akimbo and arms outstretched
Shredding the waves if that's not farfetched.

A great white was in hot pursuit
Trying to nibble at her swimsuit.
But standing tall on her shorty
Miss Ballard was tough and sporty.

Lunging forward came the great white
To chance a nibbly snappy bite.
But Miss Ballard was no kook
Whinger or sooky sook.

She used her board as a trusty shield
A teacher will never yield.
And kept the shark out of reach
There're somethings you just can't teach.

The Ponytails in Taronga Zoo
Heard the drone of a didgeredoo.
And a dingo's yelps and howls
Whines, snarls and yappy growls.

And as if by a Blue Mountains' waterfall
The Ponytails heard a kookaburra's laughing call.
And heard a galah's screech or squawk
As if on the City Tower's High Sky Walk.

And they heard a divvy van or fireys' bell
Or was it an ambo? they couldn't tell.
A million cicadas were having a hum
Or was it a hammer hitting a thumb?

Plus the crunch of a ute's gears
But could they really believe their ears?
Coz all these sounds that they heard
Were made by a lyrebird.

A big galah slipped on the stairs
Crashed into a table and four chairs.
Slid lopsided across the floor
Sliding and squawking into some more.

Ricocheting off a door without hardly trying
Sending an Esky and coolamon flying.
It had all gone wrong
What a drongo! What a nong!

Though the causes remain mysterious
It wasn't anything serious.
With nothing more than cuts and bruises
Some you win and some you loses.

The clumsy klutz just had a bingle
Nothing more, pure and simple.
But that'll hurt a bit
That's one way of putting it.

Catherine hopped like a kangaroo.
Tripped and lost a shoe.
That happens a lot down under
I shouldn't wonder.

From Tassie to the Never Never
And for no reason whatsoever.
Aussies bounce just for fun
They can't stop once they've begun.

Everywhere you've ever seen
And in every garden in between
The Aussies would put a trampoline
That's how keen the Aussies have been.

Some say the Aussie is part roo
Jacks and jills and wallabies too.
Best leave it to evolution
It's the only sensible solution.

In the Sydney Cricket Ground
It wasn't cricket the Ponytails found.
And there was a good reason
The Swans were training for next season.

With the old one-two
To me to you.
A handball give-and-go
And a free kick for a throw.

Do as you're told and stand steady
Don't argue and kick when ready.
They cleared the ball with a clean tap
And took a ping, shot and snap.

Swannies smother, spoil and bump
And jump their specky jump.
Swannies jump specky high
To shake down the thunder from the sky.

Well, stone the crows and snap me crackers
The Ponytails swung by Maccas.
They had a McSpider with loaded fries
And the same again with apple pies.

And when the arvo had nearly ended
A Hokey Pokey Shake was recommended.
The Ponytails were amped and juiced
To have this Strayan energy boost.

And when the arvo was really ended
And all the straws twisted and bended.
The Ponytails said g'day
And beaut feed, the Strayan way.

But they'd soon be peckish and pecky
And be back tomoz for brekkie.
Well, strike a light and snap me vitals
The Ponytails need subtitles.

Skippy, Skippy. Skippy the bush kangaroo
Skippy, Skippy a friend ever true.
What's that Skippy the Ponytails fell down the mine
And we're running out of time?

Come on Skip there's not a moment to lose
This sounds like a job for you roos.
Remember Skip don't be the hero
Get on the blower and dial **Triple Zero**.

I'll tell you something Skip man-to-man
This is a tricky one be as quick as you can.
Hop to it Skip as fast as you like
Through the bush d'ya need me bike?

Don't get it wrong again
I don't know how you'd explain.
Stay on the blower till you get through
Don't worry Skip, they'll know it's you.

In Glebe there were oojamaflips of many qualities
Antiquities, curiosities and dubiosities.
Ruggers, pluggers and trackie daks
All prices in Strayan including tax.

Something is special among the shonky and dinki-di
Yeah-nah, there couldn't be another within a coo-ee.
Nah-yeah, soft and smooth if a touch lopsided
They'd better take this one they all decided.

It was made chiefly of preloved scungies
Lacey and frilly grundies and undies.
Once sold in a Double Bay boutique
That was all part of the mystique.

The Ponytails bought the oojamaflip
To grace the bed of a bunyip.
And had it delivered to a bilabong
The Ponytails might've been in Oz too long.

In Luna Park the Ponytails had lots of tuck
From pop ups or a food truck.
If they'd known about the tuck in Luna
They would've turned up much, much sooner.

The Ponytails took fizzers and gummies
On the rides to fill their tummies.
But soft serve and drinks on sticks
Fairy Floss and fast rides never mix.

They got on board the Little Nipper
The Sledgehammer and Big Dipper.
The rides rattled, flew and shook
The Ponytails were feeling crook.

As the rides rolled and rumbled
Ponytail tummies growled and grumbled.
And upchucked blowing chunks
In well-turned lolly hunks.

The Ponytails saw the bidgee widgee rain
Running down their windowpane.
And as the weather turned more squally
It washed away a creepy-crawly.

It could only get wetter
Before it got any better.
Then came a sudden gutter guster
And a blowy brolly buster.

The Ponytails were ready for the big wet
That's as wet as Oz can get.
It wouldn't be better if it could get wetter
Because that's when Ponytails write a letter.

And press their noses against the glazing
Summer rain is amazing.
Then it stopped for a while
Leaving creepy-crawlies in a pile.

The Ponytails went from Woolloomooloo
Across town to Barangaroo.
And they took a shortcut
Coz the Botanical Gardens weren't shut.

Silly String, Doodle Doodle, Dilly Dilly
Wait-a-While, Wonga Wonga and Lilly Pilly
Running Postman, Smelly Socks with Hairy Panic
Stinking Roger and Billy Buttons are all botanic.

Willy Willy and Bibby Bibby
Gumbi Gumbi and Bendy Bendy.
And Duck Potato and Diddle-Dee
Are all plants too you see.

And so are Lacy Daisy and Crazy Maisy
Waddy Waddy and Jolly Holly.
Snottygobble Wattle and Floppy Flup
Oh! I might have made that last one up.

A barbie was thrown in the Ponytails' honour
To chuck cobs on the barbie if they wanna.
Or sling water balloons high and swerving
In some face most deserving.

And start a slip 'n slide with a push or shunt
And dive and glide on their rear or front.
And squirt-bottles at ten paces
Get in first and off to the races.

And run like soaker hoses
Through grass 'n beds of roses.
And let the hoses long and drippy
Make the slip 'n slide more slippy.

And a two-way sprinkler dash
Is all over in a flash.
In the BBQ they worked up an appetite
For a Boden Hall pillow fight.

And now a sort of epilogue
To end this Ponytail travelogue.
As the Boden Hall clock ticks and tocks
The Ponytails count sheep in mobs or flocks.

Soon plans would be laid
For a brand-new escapade.
But first some biff and biffo
A pillow fight for defo.

Pillows swinging on the doona
Makes brekkie time come all the sooner.
The Ponytails were in pyjamas
For dream time, no dramas.

Time enough to reminisce
And remember Sydney with their favourite Miss.
And then there was no more to say or do
Except g'night and hooroo.

End

Berlin

This Ponytail Tale was found in Berlin
Where the Ponytails had been.
Left in haste by an unsettled bill
Exactly where's a mystery still.

When these pages first appeared
They were creased, crinkled and dog-eared.
But thanks to our rigid processes
They've been put through our mangles and presses.

With their scientific procedures and secret tricks
There's nothing our team can't fix.
And they hastened to secure these files and plans
Lest they should ever fall into the wrong hands.

Perhaps we should stand to show our appreciation
Or possibly make some small donation.
But no, that would be going too far
They always knew your review would be *wunderbar*.

On a sweltering summer's day
The Ponytails sat with their feet in the Spree.
While feeding geese from the banks
As they swam past honking thanks.

But as the geese came about, so did
A bulky barge heavy and loaded.
The river flowed and water lapped
Geese honked and wings flapped.

The bargee shouldn't linger on the river
With his bulky load to deliver.
Have you nearly finished? he asked the geese politely
But that didn't seem very likely.

The geese nibbled at whatever passed by floating
From Ponytails on the bank or Berliners out boating.
The bargee gave the Ponytails a wink
He wouldn't be the first to blink.

The Ponytails had long suspected
The *Spree* and *Havel* were connected.
And arm in arm went to inspect
The very spot where they connect.

And with knees tucked under their chins
Wondered where the one stops and the other begins.
And with arms linked behind their backs
The Ponytails continued pondering rivery facts.

And then with elbows around their necks
And all questions asked with double checks.
And having cleared up any confusion
The Ponytails reached their conclusion.

Rivers intermingle, they concluded
Just like the Ponytails too did.
And wondered off giving piggybacks
That seems random but facts are facts.

The Ponytails settled under *Tiergarten* trees
For a picnic in the Berlin sun and breeze.
In the *Tiergarten* the Ponytails found just the spot
To spread out their tuck, pop and whatnot.

The Ponytails took a skipping rope
And skipped from beech to pine and pine to oak.
And two dachshunds with a long stick
Joined in their picnic skip.

And two green frogs dippy drippy
Came through the grass skippy slippy.
And two red squirrels had a scamper
Over Ponytails, doggy sticks, rope, and hamper.

Ponytails, dogs, frogs and squirrels on the pathway
You don't see that every day.
But it's good to have a get together
In Berlin's picnic weather.

Ponytails and Buddy Bears
Had a game of musical chairs.
But it's difficult to explain to a bear
You can only sit on one chair.

The bears had the chairs in a stack
Took one away and put two back.
The Ponytails finished heavy-hearted
With more chairs than when they started.

Who would have thought a Buddy Bear
Might change the rules and not play fair.
But with arms raised ready to confess
They were told, what's a chair more or less.

The Ponytails said it's all the same
And let's have another game.
It's just amazing to see
Just how fair a Ponytail and bear can be.

Long ago when Berlin was small and itty-bitty
Gates were built on the edge of the city.
But as the Berlin city grew
More and more Berliners knew.

They would have to lubricate
All the hinges on every gate.
The Ponytails liked to swing on gates
With a bag of toffees and classmates.

A squeaky gate could be annoying
And spoil a game they were enjoying.
But a game has never been spoiled
By a gate that's been well oiled.

The *Brandenburg* Gate was once on the fringes
But has never swung because it's got no hinges.
The Ponytails were sorry to see
Such a missed opportunity.

When Germans are at home
They like to play the xylophone.
The glockenspiel is also favoured
Their popularity has never wavered.

If the choice is xylophone or glockenspiel
Germans insist both have their appeal.
It's all a matter of personal preference
There's more than one frame of reference.

They play them both with mallet or stick
But the choice is yours take your pick.
Glockenspiels are made with fine German steel
And this might account for their appeal.

Xylophones, the Germans do assure us
Are made from the best wood from Honduras.
Germans play at home whenever poss
A German's home is his schloss.

As a boy, Beethoven sang soprano
But when he got older he preferred the piano.
Beethoven didn't get gigs in Bonn or Berlin
After he got croaky and couldn't sing.

He let others have a go when his voice broke
He was that sort of bloke.
But he still kept his hand in
What with conducting and composin'.

And when he was just a teenager
Beethoven wrote a sonata in D major.
And let a little time elapse
Before writing another, in F minor perhaps.

The Ponytails had to admit
Ludwig had an ear for a hit.
And could fit in a couple of bars
All his da-da-da-Daah and da-da-da-Daahs.

In the *Apfel Strudel Café alles gut* and *alles klar*
You couldn't remove a Ponytail with a crowbar.
With apples as fresh as on the tree
The *Apfel Strudel Café* is the place to be.

The Ponytails thought Kein problem and macht nix
There's no problem apple strudel can't fix.
Gute nacht and good night
There's nothing an *Apfel kuchen* can't put right.

The Ponytails asked for lots and the same again
They do that now and then.
The same again and no half measures
The bigger the better for pastry pleasures.

In the kitchen they got the feeling
They'd better start some more peeling.
One big baker's, that's what Berlin is
The Ponytails were good for bizniz.

Berlin has many treasures and the *Neus Museum*
Is a good place to see 'em.
Nefertiti always impresses
With her hats or headdresses.

But what's her hair like under her hat?
The Ponytails thought of that.
What's under that blue crown?
Is it a bun or goldy locks tumbling down?

Or ringlets springy and curly
Squeezy soft and girly.
Or fine and silky spun
And tied up in a bun.

Might she have added colour or a little tinge
And flicked and tossed her long fringe.
And if all else failed
Did she go scrunchiefied and ponytailed?

The Ponytails went to a Peacock Island ball
Like so many in Boden Hall.
In fancy dress to masquerade
It was the latest Ponytail escapade.

Catherine was asked for a dance by a prince
I know! It hasn't happened since.
Catherine accepted red-faced
And was whisked on the dance floor giddy-paced.

Beneath twinkling stars and moonlight
And on the stroke of midnight.
The Ponytails had to leave
In a great hurry some believe.

And now a slipper fell on a palace stair
Like a sparkling clue it sparkled there.
The Ponytails were in disguise
But only Catherine's slippers were her size... ...

A haus frau is much accustomed
To bake a cake for her husband.
And a Ponytail is inclined
To lick the spoon we do find.

Birds pecking bread in the garden
Say it's soft at first but quick to harden.
And a dachshund can tell with a sniff
If it's still soft or gone stiff.

Remember if they get dropped in the yard
Biscuits go soft and cakes go hard.
And whether you have the wings of a dove,
Watching the yard from high above

Or the tail of a dirty old crow,
That's always good to know.
And any bird proud to be a Berliner
Would have the lot for dinner.

The *Reichstag* has a glass dome on the roof
It's leak, damp and rainproof.
The dome is always well maintained
But anything could happen if it rained.

What if a catch were broken
And a window flung wide open?
And the water flowed and got in
What would they say about that in Berlin?

If the dome filled with rainwater
Sploshing around like it didn't ought a?
It only takes someone to mishandle
A dome window and cause a scandal.

The Ponytails could be up to their necks
That's what happens if no one checks.
And the *Reichstag* could have a flooded lid
Lucky it never did.

The Ponytails thought it wunderbar
To see Berlin from a little car.
And were chuffed to cram in a Trabant
That were becoming so scarce and scant.

More Ponytails than ever before
Got in the Trabant and closed the door.
They would've put that in a records book
If a judge had been there to look.

Putt-putt-putt, according to the tittle-tattle
Went the little auto with its quirky rattle.
And splutter, splutter with a misfire
And wobble, wobble on a flat tyre.

And bangs and knocks and rat-a-tat-tats
All the way to *Alexander Platz*.
With smoke, clangs and clangour
Twice round the square went the banger.

The Ponytails never forget the code
For crossing a busy Berlin road.
And have never had any objections
To looking carefully in both directions.

Sometimes there's a signal and sometimes not
But the code must never be forgot.
Links, rechts, links - dann ist alles fix!
And over you go in two ticks.

Signals allow ample time to get across
The little rot or grün mann is boss.
Just remember the little *mann* knows
On rot he stops and on *grün* he goes.

The Ponytails began
By waiting for the little *mann*.
But never asked, where did you get that hat?
He gets a lot of that.

Another way for the Ponytails to get around
Was on the Berlin underground.
And stood scuffled and shuffled as most did
Shoulder to shoulder and overcrowded.

But before manoeuvres were completed
The Ponytails were hoping to be seated.
And wondered whether
They could all sit together.

The U-Bahn stopped with squeals and breaking
Jolts, rattles and shuddery shaking.
Doors snapped open with a hiss
But getting a seat could be hit or miss.

They saw the seats much awaited
Tatty and patched but vacated.
Then off they took with a screech
With a Ponytail in a seat each.

A Rottweiler was frantically scratching her ear
A Doberman was watching but didn't interfere.
He thought it best to avoid such things as these
And let her rely on her expertise.

The rottweiler had the physique
For the rapid hind leg strum technique.
She'd know her own itch best
The Doberman looked on, most impressed.

A scratch like this doesn't happen every day
She was digging deep and well on her way.
Nothing could stop her once she got going
But when she'd stop there was no knowing.

The Rottweiler gave it one last thump
Now, if only she could reach her rump.
The Doberman walked off with a jaunty spring
He knew he'd done the right thing.

Kaiser Bill often felt like he
Would wear a helmet high and spiky.
The Kaiser could carry off a spiky hat
You have to give him that.

And so's not to get caught in a chandelier.
He'd have his batman shout, All clear!
If the Ponytails had been his advisor
He might have been a wiser Kaiser.

But Kaiser Bill was allowed his quirks
Being Kaiser had its perks.
He liked to be booted and suited
Cheered, revered and saluted.

Kaiser Bill was always smart and snazzy snappy
That's what made him happy.
And he liked a new medal and a makeover
That was Kaiser Bill all over.

On Schönhauser Allee the Ponytails saw
Artsy graffiti bold and raw.
And on the same *straße*, where it's legal
A street artist was painting a German eagle.

He called miss Balard, *meine* sweety
And asked her to help with his graffiti.
She joined in with his crew
It would be rude not to.

She started with squiggles and rings
Rolling over the eagle's wings.
And painted squiggly scrawls
Sprayed up high on the Berlin walls.

And soon had her tags on display
Where you can still see them today.
Among phrases coined sweet and nice
And some much more colourful advice.

Ostriches in Tier Park zoo
Thought hello, this is new.
As Ponytails hung high in a cable car
Over where the ostriches are.

And looked up in a quizzical manner
You don't see that on the Savannah.
And bowed low and swayed
With wings and feathers all displayed.

Then the Ponytails heard a booming sound
Coming up from the ostrich compound.
And with a bow and sway
Began to dance the ostrich way.

And with their deep shoulder action
The Ponytails got an ostrichy reaction.
Both ostriches and Ponytails in the zoo
Began to do the do-si-do.

And now a sort of epilogue
To complete this Ponytail travelogue.
Soon their trip would be over
They'll be on the train and back to Dover.

As the Boden Hall clock chimes through the night
I know what you'd do and you'd be right.
You'd have a pillow in each hand
And be swinging like an oompah band.

Funny enough and as luck would have it
The Ponytails were of the same habit.
Fully loaded and looking grim
The Ponytails were going in.

There'd be time enough to reminisce
And remember Berlin with their favourite Miss.
Soon plans would be laid
For a brand-new escapade.

Ende

ODD JOB

Two bobbies parked late at night
Switched off the engine and the light.
They settled down with two coffees
Puzzle books and a bag of toffees.

But would they have the patience
For this nocturnal surveillance?
Their sergeant had her doubts
If they were up to these stakeouts.

Would they stay alert?
Two more coffees wouldn't hurt.
The lamplight flickered and the lamplight glowed
A stray cat crossed the road.

The bobbies stretched and the bobbies yawned
Not long now before it dawned.
Just rest their eyes but not for long
Just a few minutes and prove 'em all wrong.

An au pair was overloaded with the shopping
And the little boy she was dropping.
Things were looking bad
She couldn't hold on to the lad.

She remembered the words of his mother
To look after him like her little brother.
But she was losing her grip
The toddler was beginning to slip.

He was squirming and dropping fast
He was a help at first but it didn't last.
With runny nose, dribbling and snotty
And now he was demanding the potty

The au pair was struggling with the nipper
His buttons, fastener and zipper.
The snotty kid was wriggling and kicking
Wriggles, kicks and nose picking.

A librarian frowned and raised a finger to her lips
Then raised and steepled her fingertips.
She rested her chin on one fist
And gave her bracelet a little twist.

She checked her nails and glanced at her watch
It was time to turn her frown up a notch.
She fixed her gaze and shrugged a shoulder
Till her frown became a smoulder.

She approached slowly hugging books
Shooting glances and stern looks.
She closed her eyes and nodded no
Read in silence or off you go.

She flicked her fringe towards the door
As if to say, out you go if there's anymore.
She returned to her desk with her head held high
Library rules must apply.

A spy's cover was blown
He was out in the cold and on his own.
The spy was working for the other side
He said he was on theirs but he lied.

It had been a game of double bluff
Of microdots, codes and stuff.
And secret cameras in buttonholes
Sleeper cells, never tells and moles.

But deep cover had been getting lonely
With so much bumf for your eyes only.
It wasn't completely unexpected
When he was rumbled and defected.

He had to wriggle through barbed wire
And under the stars to avoid gunfire.
He'd been leading a double life
How would he explain to the wife?

A tailor had fallen on hard times
But had a plan for window signs.
Could his run of bad luck be broken
With a sign saying English Spoken?

That's the way to improve trade
And sell more of the suites he made.
He quickly wrote the sign himself
And placed it on a window shelf.

Would English be as hard as it looks?
The tailor started with records and books.
The book said, speak English in just nine days
By repeating the words and then the phrase.

The tailor was sowing and cutting along chalk lines
Ready to repeat phrases over and over many times.
But the first lesson caused a hitch
Repeat after me, *My tailor is rich!*

A detectorist was detecting in sweeps
Listening for lucky blips and beeps.
He was hoping to find coins of gold or copper
Dropped by some clumsy ancient shopper.

They're often hidden among bones and stones
And detected with headphones' beeping tones.
They're waiting to be lifted with his spade
And put in a museum to be displayed.

The detectorist was searching for precious metal
But this time only found part of a kettle.
Still, that's better than his usual handful
Of ring pulls by the bagful.

Treasure is an unusual anomaly
It's not what you find commonly.
The detectorist continued to move slowly toward
The first sign of a hidden hoard.

A landlady had a room free
With a bouncy bed and views of the sea.
And a sign saying, *management regret's*
No refund's, no children, no noise, no pet's.

Burnt toast and a burnt sausage
Cold tea and hairs in the porridge.
Scrambled egg all wishy-washy
The milk's off and there's no coffee.

Cooking in rooms is out of the question
That's a no, the very suggestion.
After dark there's a shout
Get to bed and lights out!

Breakfast finishes at nine
The breakfast room had another sign.
I do like to be beside the seaside
Another day in paradise the landlady sighed.

The coal miner intended
To catch Canary before his shift ended.
But flying up and down the shaft
Canary fluttered and whistled past.

No-one could stop Canary popping out
For his chirpy fly about.
He was just flapping and stretching his wings
Canary flies Canary sings.

Half bird and half bat
There's nothing you can do about that.
Canaries change and canaries vary
You never know with a canary.

Canary flutters Canary hops
Canary pops on beams and props.
Canary sings Canary flies
Canary dreams of blue skies.

A detective thought a name rang a bell
But where had he heard it before? he couldn't tell.
Who was that? What did he do?
Search me I haven't a clue.

The detective knew he knew that face
But couldn't think of the time or place.
Something niggled in his brain
He had a hunch he couldn't explain.

What was that face concealing?
He had an inkling he had a feeling.
He was on to something but couldn't be sure
Where had he seen that face before?

He'd have to check the mugshots
Go through the records and join up the dots.
Yes, that's it! Half a mo. hold on
No, no it's gone.

Matron was in the linen cupboard smoothing sheets
Running her hands over creases, folds and pleats.
It was a cubbyhole of pats and strokes
Not a world much explored by blokes.

It was where a gentle squeeze
Might release apple blossom or sea breeze.
And a little sniff may suggest or hint
Of lavender or peppermint.

It was a defiant retreat or outpost
Out of bounds to most.
It was where Matron's muffled rustles
Blended with her sniffs and shuffles.

In the linen cupboard stood Matron
Half cotton, half wool and starched apron.
Patting the items in their places
Comforting sheets and pillowcases.

A barista chose a classically blended
For a customer she'd just befriended.
I was a trainee not long ago
Would you like to have a go?

She told him how it works
Making friends are the perks.
Two shots in regular and three in large
With a slight adjustment to the charge.

A *latte* is bigger than an *espresso*
A *cortado* is too but less so.
With a large you get a long spoon
And you can stay all afternoon.

Then she turned to do her job
Pulled a handle and turned a knob.
And with a hiss from the coffee machine
She disappeared in the hissy steam.

An auctioneer held up the first lot
Have a look it's the best we've got.
It's a type of veez, vaze or vase
That once belonged to the czar of czars.

There's no damage to mention
Nothing that needs your attention.
It's never too severe
According to the auctioneer.

Just a tiny hairline crack
Goes around the front and back.
Then it curls up and down
It doesn't show if you turn it round.

And a tiny chip you can hardly see
It's best not to look if you ask me.
That's what it's like with pots and jars
It was good enough for the czars.

A traffic warden was issuing fines
Five cars had parked on the lines.
Nearly a whole inch over and a tyre flat
He wasn't having that.

He was sticking the tickets on the windscreens
Under the wipers where they would be seen.
They'd have to pay quick or there'd be trouble
A day late and they'd have to pay double.

The fine doubles that's inflation
This official had a reputation.
Lines are crossed and lines are blurred
Fines are doubled you must've heard.

But he got in a muddle
And dropped the fines in a puddle.
Five cars splashed him for a joke
It couldn't have happened to a nicer bloke.

A technician was twisting wires
Snipping and clipping with clippers and pliers.
Checking the wiring and the switches
Looking for faults, bugs and glitches.

The system was colour coded
So it wouldn't get overloaded.
But there'd been smoke and flashes
Funny noises and loud crashes.

The technician checked the amps, volts and watts
Buttons, dials and fuse box.
He checked the sockets and the plug
There was still no sign of a bug.

There were power surges and fuses blown
For many reasons all unknown.
That's the trouble with hi-tech
He would have to double check.

A teacher was quietly chalking
He'd insisted on no talking.
But a girl screamed in shock
When a spider climbed up her sock.

Stop that! don't scream anymore
Have you never seen a spider before?
But that was the end of the quiet
The class was starting to riot.

Silence! no more fuss
That's not like us.
But it was running up her leg and skirt
Stop that screaming it can't hurt.

But now the spider was in the girl's hair
And was flicked and shaken where
It landed on the teacher who with a twirl
Screamed louder than the girl.

A ski instructor was on his skis
Demonstrating his expertise.
Do *ze* same just like me
Do you see?

Put *ze* weight on *ze* right skiii
And bend ze other knee.
Now shift *ze* weight to the other side
And keep *ze* legs open wide.

Keep *ze* arms straight in between
Do you see what I mean?
Hold on tight and don't let go
Do you follow?

But a mist hung heavy in the air
Hello, hello. Are you there?
There's no need for alarm
Hello, hello. I can't see my arm.

A beekeeper was by his hive
Waiting for the bees to arrive.
They had never been so late
The beekeeper had to wait.

A bee can't be hurried
But he was getting worried.
They never take this long
Something must be wrong.

The boys all stayed home with the queen
He always knew where they'd been.
It was the girls who were out in no hurry
He couldn't help but worry.

It was very late when he heard them coming
With a buzzy buzz and distant humming.
This wouldn't be their first warning
He would have words in the morning.

A farmer was in a field of lambs
With bleating sheep and the rams.
He put the sheep in a sheep pen
Bath day had come around again.

Shorn and sheared, ready to be dipped.
The sheep were waiting to be tipped.
The ewes were patiently waiting their turn
But the rams were pushy, they never learn.

Tut-tut-tut the farmer tutted
As the rams pushed and butted.
Then the farmer pulled a pulley
And dropped in a woolly bully.

While little lambs may gambol and frolic
Through pesticide and carbolic.
Rams are much more at ease
With their ticks, lice and fleas.

A prison guard was on his knees
Looking under tables for his keys.
They should've been chained to his belt
Not under the table where he knelt.

But if they weren't there or in the canteen
He couldn't think where else he'd been.
He'd looked all over the clink
Where they could be he couldn't think.

They might be under a flowerpot
He couldn't remember, he forgot.
Or hid under a garden gnome
Like he always did at home.

They could've been left in E Block
If he couldn't find them, he'd have to knock.
But there was no reply from the inmates
Where'd they go? Who opened the gates?

A lifeguard was on patrol
The tide was out but you never know.
Someone could be taken by an ocean wave
There's always someone to save.

If seas get rough and choppy
And decks get slippery and sloppy.
Something could happen untoward
Someone could splosh overboard.

But could it be too far to swim?
The pier was far enough for him.
If he couldn't swim no more
Perhaps they would drift ashore.

How quickly a poor swimmer
Could become a shark's dinner.
The alarm was sounded to screams and shouts
In he went he had no doubts.

A racing driver came out the pits
Not the fastest he admits.
He'd never crashed in a race
But slowed down just in case.

He spent too long in a pit stop
Asking if it looks like rain or not.
And chatting about race conditions
Tyre pressure and front positions.

There was a space or what he calls a gap
Getting bigger and bigger with every lap.
Again and again he was overtaken
And by the back marker if he wasn't mistaken.

But at Le Mans, Monaco or the Indy
In Maserati, Ferrari or Lamborghini.
In Monza, Imola or Brands Hatch
He always finished without a scratch.

A children's entertainer was modelling balloons
Playing the banjo and painting cartoons.
Card tricks are what he did best
But the kids weren't impressed.

Where's the lady you cut in half?
Cut her up and give us a laugh.
Where's she gone? they wanted to know
We want some chopping not the banjo.

Are balloons and cartoons all you've got?
Shuffling and dealing and all that rot.
My mate's mum is game
Saw her up or the other one, it's all the same.

I don't dare do that no more
I can't do it like I did before.
But let's give it just one more try
Hop in and tell me if the box is dry.

A soldier arrived in his jeep
With a cheery hooty tooty beep.
He drove in through the gate
Very ambitious but a little late.

The soldier's day had begun
With a cold shower and a run.
He was up early polishing his boots
IIe knew the drill for new recruits.

Stamping his feet and standing at ease
He'd just arrived and was eager to please.
He knew he could soon be driving tanks
Getting promotion and climbing the ranks.

He could reach those dizzy heights
He had the sergeant's job in his sights.
But he was peeling spuds and guarding latrines
Learning what zero eight hundred hours means.

A footballer was limbering up
It was his big chance in the cup.
He was having a prematch ponder
He was focused but his mind could wander.

He knew his chances were slender
To bend the ball past a defender.
Perhaps the defenders would all be bandy
Three nutmegs would come in handy.

Perhaps the referee would stop play
Give a free kick and see it his way?
With a bit of luck and the right decision
The team could move up a division.

Perhaps he would chance a scissor kick
Score again and again and get a hat-trick.
The sky was the limit until
They went down three nil.

A dinner lady was confused and flustered
Was it a pot of mustard or was it custard?
I thought I would know by the colour or smell
But I've been sniffing for ages and still can't tell.

I don't want to get it wrong
Get mixed up and put the wrong one on.
It's me who gets the blame
If the puds don't taste the same.

I can't have the custard thin and runny
It's on me if the pud tastes a bit funny.
I have my reputation I got the OBE
The royals were here to pin it on me.

But you're only as good as your last pud
Mustard on me crumble and that's me knighthood.
I'll have to make another lot
And keep me eye on the pot.

A zookeeper will always sweep
Softly while the lions sleep.
He sweeps the lions' cage twice nightly
On tippy toes and very quietly.

Sweeping as quietly as a mouse
The zookeeper sweeps the lion house.
He sweeps around and in between
And likes to keep the cages clean.

He doesn't like mucky paws
Mucking up his clean floors.
He can't relax or rest unless
He's cleaned up the lions' mess.

A lion may sleep and a lion may roar
But they like to wake up to a clean floor.
Thank you for sweeping the cages and floors
You scratch my back and I'll scratch yours.

A model was pausing to do a catwalk pose
Twisting and turning to show off her clothes.
With a low neckline worn off the shoulder
And head held high like they told her.

Then she slips in and out of a dress
And does a quick change unless
She tries something else instead
And someone pulls it off over her head.

In high heels or sensible shoes
Up and down in ones and twos.
She pouts and sulks for no reason
It's what they all do this season.

A fashion show never fails
To end in a frenzy of sales.
Or the lot's sold under the hammer
You can't put a price on glamour.

A horse trainer needed a winner
But his little filly was just a beginner.
How could she stand a chance
Against bigger horses from Ireland and France?

But it all depends
She's very fast on the bends.
A big stallion is all hooves and nervy
Where a little filly is sleek and curvy.

The French could find it heavy going
Soft and sticky there was no knowing.
Or the going could be good
Then the Irish would struggle, so they would.

For this horse trainer
The two thirty was a no-brainer.
Under starters orders came runners and riders
Neck and neck were favourites and outsiders.

A drummer was banging out a beat.
Swinging arms and drumming feet.
Among party goers and party mingles
Bashing drums and crashing cymbals.

Drums beat loud drums beat bold
The foundations shook, rattled and rolled.
Neighbours complained and banged back
Walls and ceilings began to crack.

Floorboards bounced and plaster split
Drums four to the floor he wouldn't quit.
Neighbours began to compete
Louder and louder came the double beat.

That's the way many a song goes
With tom-toms and driving bongos.
Knocking on ceilings at right angles
With umbrellas and broom handles.

A lawyer stood up in court and held his lapels
The accused was brought up from the cells.
Well, m'lud, it's a tragic story
Of felony and outlawry.

But never mind if he robbed or shot or not.
Let us consider the sentence he got.
The evidence and his confession are duly noted
But that's a year for every shot if he hadn't reloaded.

It's not a question of clemency or anything of that
sort
Let's give him a second chance, may it please the
court.
But it didn't please the judge
He stuck to his guns and wouldn't budge.

The judge adjusted his wig and gown
And banged his gavel, take him down.
It'll be a long time before he's free
Lock him up and throw away the key.

A newscaster was making it clear
These were the events of the year.
The stakes couldn't be any higher
This was going down to the wire.

This was the end of an era
He couldn't make it any clearer.
We're all in the firing line
We're running out of time.

It's an all-time high and low
This could be touch and go.
We could all go up in smoke
Let's go live to some ordinary bloke.

I think we should look at the cold hard facts
The whole country is on the brink of collapse.
What we need is a line in the sand
Get round the table and make a stand.

A nurse was taking the patient's pulse
It was much too high would he convulse?
I think he's still with us he understands
Don't worry mate you're in safe hands.

He might need a scan
She'll arrange it and off she ran.
Was his heart racing could he wait?
She'll be back hold on mate.

These symptoms could be rare
Give him a suck of gas and air.
He could have a fever or a fit
Suck this mate you'll make it.

What did you eat last?
He didn't reply was he sinking fast?
No, it's not too late
They've never lost a mate.

A hotel receptionist had the bill prepared
No expense had been spared.
Valet parking for your bike
Double order of those burgers you like.

A private box on race day
Tickets to see your team play.
Morning paper and breakfast in bed
Cancelled taxi and limo instead.

Sunken bath with city view
Let's see what that all comes to.
Yes, it does seem a lot
But I think there's something I forgot.

To all this we must add
A dozen flights from the helipad.
Hold on! Aren't you the boy from the other day
Who got kicked out cos he couldn't pay?

A barber was twitching with his razor waving
Should this barber really be shaving?
A customer was waiting for a shave
Nerves of steel he was very brave.

Covered in foam and shaving gel
With a dab of cologne cos he liked the smell.
Don't worry I can hold it steady
Let me know when you're ready.

Shaving's what I like most
Come here I'll get in close.
Oh, yes. This is fun.
A couple more scrapes and you'll be done.

He was in the hands of his barber
Hold on I've got one sharper.
With every twitch his confidence grew
Just don't move whatever you do.

A dentist was having a bad day
With toothache and tooth decay.
It was a day of drill and fill, rinse and spit
And then a crown wouldn't fit.

The dentist's usual twist and press
Had stuck it on more or less.
But then with a rinse and suck
It popped off and came unstuck.

The dentist couldn't charge since
The crown came off in the rinse.
But the dentist remembered his training
And stopped the patient from complaining.

This is what we call the release and rise
It's because you're an awkward size.
It's caused by your warp and texture
I'm afraid I'll have to charge you extra.

A secretary was having a moan
Shouting *oiga, oiga* down the phone.
And *dígame dígame* for good measure
She was under a lot of pressure.

The young lady had the suspicion
It wasn't a person who wouldn't listen.
I don't think you know what I mean
Are you a person or a machine?

And could you speak a bit slower?
I can't keep up on the blower.
Could you repeat that please?
Did you speak or did you sneeze?

Sorry, I can't keep track
I'll have to call you back.
Or will you hang up and call again?
What is it you do in Spain?

A cook was stirring a big stew pot
Under steamy clouds and bubbly hot.
With a dash of chili sauce and garlic powder
She turned up the heat and it bubbled louder.

She tried a sip from her wooden spoon
But was it ready, was it too soon?
Ah! that's just what I thought
It needs another pinch of salt.

The delicate aroma was appreciated
The cook sniffed, stirred and waited.
Do you recognise that smell?
Do you know what that is, can you tell?

You're not allowed to know
But I'll give you a clue it begins with o.x.oh!
That's my mum's secret recipe
You'll never get that out of me.

A tourist guide saying follow me
Was pointing far out to sea.
That's where it all occurred
Over there, that's what I heard.

Can you see? have a good look
It's all in the guidebook.
It was a mighty force
There's nothing there now, of course.

There were gunboats or men-of-war I think
Those ones that are easy to sink.
They had plenty to shoot at
I remember that.

I'm not good with names or places
I'm much better with faces.
It happened in July or November
It's a lot to remember.

A postman was climbing the stairs
There was no lift but who cares?
There's the postman's vow and the postman's oath
This postman swore 'em both.

And there's the postman's golden rule
That he learned in postman school.
A postman's word is true
The mail must get through.

On his days off he wrote letters
To Simonas, Ramonas and Henriettas.
He liked to keep in touch with them
And dropped 'em a line now and again.

For a pen pal there's nothing worse
Than not receiving a letter in prose or verse.
And it's so much better
If the postman delivers his own letter.

The sheriff wasn't quick on the draw
But fast or slow the law's the law.
It was time to clean up this town
The sheriff was having a crackdown.

With his Stetson set at an oblique angle
And spurs turning with a jangle.
He gave the saloon doors a push
And stepped inside to the hush and shush.

A gunslinger stood up and went for his gun
Whirled it around his finger till it twirled and spun.
He stepped in and out of his lasso and began
A Texas two-step around the law man.

Hello, thought the sheriff, I wasn't expecting that
And he adjusted the angle of his hat.
Should he go for his gun on the off chance
Or join in with the dance?

A cleaner was on the top floor
She had to get away by four.
The dusting was done and dusted
But the dishwasher was broken and busted.

And a stack of washing up in the sink
Meant she might need a rethink.
She took off her rubber gloves with a snap
And reached for her thinking cap.

An add said if you're ever in a jam
Count on me, I'm your man.
No job too big or small
Appliances fixed give me a call.

With mop shouldered and bucket in hand
Things could still go as planned.
If only she could get the man
To drop her off in his van.

A superhero woke up in the small hours
With even more superpowers.
He could scream and no-one would hear
And make monsters disappear.

His night vision was working well
So too was his super smell.
But with monsters reappearing every night
He couldn't sleep without the light.

As free as a bird he would swan
Around school with no clothes on.
Or battle in epic dramas
In his Superman pyjamas.

In the morning every demon had fled
He couldn't find any under the bed.
With his enemies all squashed and flattened
He was trying to remember what happened.

A coastguard was contacting a yacht
Come in! Come in! Are you receiving me or not?
The seas are getting choppy
Over! Over! Do you copy?

The winds are light
In German Bite.
But getting erratic
By Scilly Automatic.

It'll soon be blowing gale force
Over! Over! Can you alter course?
Hold on to your hat
If you can't do that.

Hold up, just a sec
Half a mo, I'll double check.
No, no, I was right
Your best bet is German Bite.

A jewel thief was casing the joint
He could've got the plans but what's the point.
He always relied on the stereotype
His stripy jumper and a drainpipe.

He was busy lock picking
When an alarm lit up and started ticking.
Now he would have to work fast
One more minute is all he asked.

But he knew his boyish charm
Could get around any alarm.
He left with the swag over his shoulder
Leaving a single rose for the owner.

And a glass of bubbly champagne
Then a quick getaway on the boat train.
He would always leave in style
Rome tonight, tomorrow the Nile.

An MP was working late
In the House for a debate.
Yet more nitpicking and all-night sitting
Banging doors, division bells and hair splitting.

Order! Order! I can't hear a word
The honourable member must be heard.
Order! Order! Cried the Speaker
But his voice was getting weaker.

Will the member in a sedentary position
Stop interrupting the opposition?
Shouts of nays and yeas at this late hour
Rang out along the corridors of power.

Understanding order number 43
And the power given to me.
The backbencher must withdraw
Out you go and don't slam the door.

A wine taster had a sip of the Beaujolais
Tilted his head and considered the bouquet.
He swilled it between his teeth
Over his tongue and underneath.

He was getting hints of blackberry
And whispers of lime and cherry.
He could taste the forest floor
Wet leaves and soft straw.

With undertones of cedar and oak
And a touch of moss and distant smoke.
Unveiling layers, full-bodied and oaky
An alluring array, complex and smoky.

He snapped his fingers to underline
His appreciation of the wine.
And then spat it out in a gobby manner
Wine tasting isn't all glamour.

A customs officer picked up a book
And held it up for a squinty look.
Then his look became a stare
Could there be anything to declare?

He held the book up to his ear
Books are not always as they appear.
Then he waved it under his nose
Closed his eyes, the training shows.

There was something about it he couldn't ignore
He'd seen one like this somewhere before.
Was it carried by a man in a beret
And a false beard or toupee?

He gave it one more knowing look
Listened, sniffed and shook.
But further inspection would have to wait
He'd better get off to work or he'd be late.

A pilot's departure was delayed
By mist and fog but he was unafraid.
He was taxiing down the runway
Ready for take-off anyway.

But the fog was closing in quicker
The murk was getting thicker and thicker.
Fog hangs heavy and fog clings
The pilot couldn't see the wings.

He carried out a preflight check
And radioed the tower, he was hi-tech.
Bravo, Lima, Tango, Charlie
Romeo, Foxtrot, where are we?

Hello, hello. United Flight 780
The fog is lifting we're going to let you go.
It's clear skies to Honolulu
If only I were going with you.

An actor dropped a prop and missed his cue
Forgot his lines and made the audience boo.
He was having a very bad day
Speaking lines for the wrong play.

If only he could big up his part
And get more lines, it'd be a start.
If only he could remember the ones he had
Things wouldn't be so bad.

If he didn't get stage fright
Lose the script and trip over a light.
Fluff his lines and have to mime
Ad lib making it up all the time.

Did the audience booing
Have to be his undoing?
No, if he didn't make another mistake
This could be his big break.

A lock keeper pushed on the beam
And opened the gate to go downstream.
To the surprise of the lock keeper
The lock was filled with a minesweeper.

The lock keeper looked on in disbelief
Could you lend a hand? cried the chief.
We seem to have gone off course
Have you seen anything of the strike force?

We have to rendezvous at zero eight hundred
Thanks, anyway. I just wondered.
Not to worry, I'll send up a flare
Do you happen to have one spare?

Or I'll get a signal off in code
I'll soon have us back on the road.
The chief asked the lock keeper to point the way
It was going to be a very long day.

A lollipop lady stood her ground
Holding up her yellow sign with red surround.
A driver will always stop
When he sees the lollipop

And let the kids cross the road.
According to the highway code.
A young lady came hoping by
With one sock wet and one sock dry.

Asking, has anyone found a shoe?
I don't know, what's a girl to do?
I can't think where it could be
What am I like? that's just like me.

Drivers beeped and drivers frowned
Would this shoe ever be found?
Heads were shaken and heads were shook
Till drivers got out their cars and helped her look.

A mechanic promised to mend
An old banger for a friend.
It'd once been one of the greats
He could fix it up for mates' rates.

He would have to straighten the axle and differential
And four remoulds would be essential.
He had a couple of wheels with some tread
And two more out back in the shed.

A little more air would be a must
And a quick rub of sandpaper to clear the rust.
Perhaps he could tune her up a bit
He'd have to see what's in his tool kit.

It had been a good runner in its heyday
But was now in need of a respray.
He could buff out the dents and scratches
And repaint the doors so everything matches.

A vet slipped behind the screen
This procedure would be routine.
The dog was fighting fit and in good shape
But he was in for the snip, there was no escape.

With lots of distractions to put him at his ease
He was panting and wagging and eager to please.
He was offered choccy biccies or rubber chews
He jumped on the table with nothing to lose.

The vet made an incision
Biccies or chews? it was a big decision.
Despite pills and needles he would stay awake
Biccies or chews? there was a lot at stake.

He was soon dreaming in recovery
Of chasing rabbits in the shrubbery.
He wouldn't go back to his old habits
From now on he would stick to rabbits.

A woodcutter swung as hard as he could
At the tallest tree in the wood.
But there was no way to tell
How long this giant would take to fell.

And his fears were well founded
When his chopper just rebounded.
But the woodcutter kept swinging nonstop
And swung all day to give this tree the chop.

He kept chop chopping all day
Until the tree started to give way.
The blade was getting hotter and hotter
At last, the tree began to teeter and totter.

Timber! cried the woodcutter
With his heart all aflutter.
We might have to wait a bit
Hold up! No, I think that's it.

A water diviner walked along a ditch
When her divining rod began to twitch.
There was something there underground
Flowing but not showing, what had she found?

This could mean only one thing
She must be on top of a spring.
Or perhaps a cool babbling brook
She dug a hole to have a look.

Then her fingers began to quiver
She'd have to go deeper it could be a river.
And then looking up from down there
She saw a Mad Hatter and a March Hare.

They were pouring tea from a big teapot
Until it was poured and flowed a lot.
Soon there was an overflow which
Babbled up and filled the ditch.

A greengrocer's boy was getting the hang
Of throwing a banana like a boomerang.
And he could juggle carrots and bananas
As well as raisins and sultanas.

And he could roll a melon across the floor
Hitting a sprout or apple core.
And turn a parsnip or some such root
Into a whistle or perky flute.

All alone in the back store
He was playing games and keeping score.
With the fruit and veg lying in bits
He'd have one more game, double or quits.

The greengrocer was unimpressed
With his world record and personal best.
Saying, Come on me lad you're not 'ere t'play
But he'd give a high five at the end of the day.

A florist had gone organic
But greenfly had her in a panic.
Traps, soapy spray and swot
The florist had tried the lot.

If only there were someway
To keep the pesky pests at bay.
Surely a quick spurt and squirt
Of something insecticidal wouldn't hurt.

Perhaps a whiff of repellent
Would be the best deterrent.
A greenfly wouldn't know how to hide
From squirts and spurts of insecticide.

With two spray guns of pest control
The florist was ready to rock n roll.
She'd soon have 'em wheezing and sneezing
And holding their noses tight and squeezing.

A trouble shooter came up short
The trouble was worse than he thought.
He'd given it his best shot
He'd racked his brains and pondered a lot.

A problem solver found the problem tough
She'd done her best but enough was enough.
She wasn't afraid to admit
It was time to give up and quit.

An ideas man couldn't find the solution
To solve the problem and reach a conclusion.
He couldn't explain the ins and outs
He had so many nagging doubts.

Things aren't always as easy as they appear
Things can get tricky but never fear.
Never worry about being quick
Because nobody likes a clever Dick.

A writer thought he could write a best seller
Cos, he knew grammar and was a good speller
And then after that he would
Write another just as good.

He could be artful, crafty and cunning
And write the twisty bits you didn't see coming.
His mystery novel would consist
Of a surprising ending with a twist.

A snazzy cover and catchy title
And an ads campaign would be vital.
A jazzy cover and no messing
And a plot to keep 'em guessing.

And then he would quote
From the book what he wrote.
Uplifting words to inspire
Every reader and book buyer.

A school prefect was in her new blazer
A little girl was late, if only she had a taser.
Prefect told her to come along and get moving
And stared at her disapproving.

She made a note in her little black book
And gave the girl a closer look.
Where's your tie? she inquired
Why aren't you in the uniform required?

And your skirt is too short
I'm putting you on report.
You know that's not what we wear
Prefect was always firm but fair.

Pull up your socks and tuck in your shirt
A comb through your hair wouldn't hurt.
Then Prefect was called by a classmate
Come quick we're going to be late.

A schoolgirl was put on report
She was standing up straight as she'd been taught.
Accused of being a school tie refuser
She'd come to face her accuser.

The young lady was outspoken
Rules are made to be broken.
I never wear a tie oddly enough
And I don't comb my hair cos I'm a scruff.

I like my socks at half mast
Like Pippi Longstocking in the past.
And short skirts are best I've always thunk
Not everyone can rock my funk.

And shirt out or shirt in
I think it's all win-win.
And after that little tiff
Off she flounced with a loud sniff.

A personal trainer was huffing and puffing
To work off the pies he'd been stuffing.
But no matter how hard he tries
He still looks stuffed full of pies.

He'd just have to work off
All those pies he shouldn't scoff.
He was trying to think thin
Take a deep breath and hold it in.

But it was too late for half measures
He'd have to pay for his simple pleasures.
Once again, he'd have to feel the burn
Would he never learn?

He checked his weight that same night
But hold fast, that can't be right.
He tipped the scales without warning
Four kilos more than in the morning.

A forklift driver was a little miffed
At being alone on the night shift.
If there's one thing he hates
It's working alone without his mates.

Where had they all gone?
Leaving him alone with his off and on.
And his lever for up and down
And the wheel to turn around.

But now he had the aisles to himself
Taking what he liked from any shelf.
He'd never seen what was on the very top
Or around the back where you can't stop.

Now he was free to explore
The places he hadn't been before.
From loading dock to delivery bay
With no-one to get in his way.

A clown on a fire engine with bells ringing
Arrived with hoses and buckets swinging.
Raising the ladder higher and higher
He was racing to put out the fire.

The brakes came on with a slam
And the doors blew off with a bang.
With holes in the buckets and flat tyres
It wouldn't be easy to put out fires.

With trousers too big and baggy
And shoes too long and flappy.
Something always goes wrong
He wouldn't stay dry for long.

The clown was sitting in the water puddled
Arms around his bucket empty and cuddled.
But then dropped in the clown's tear and sob
He would have to find a new job.

It was time for the teacher to face facts
Perhaps he had been a little lax.
It was time to put his foot down with a firm hand
And make those girls understand.

He would treat them all the same
No-one was really more to blame.
But they would have to be told
He had the rules to uphold.

He would call for silence and explain
How they mustn't do that again.
Yes, they'd have to promise not to do that anymore
No, that' no good; he'd been double crossed before.

Had the girls been underestimated?
Perhaps prefect could step up if delegated.
But was he really being realistic
With his head in curlers and covered in lipstick?

A char lady was on the final straight
She was getting closer, not long to wait.
With her trolly and all her supplies on
Appeared the char lady on the horizon.

With buns at just a few pence
Iced and glazed, hang the expense.
Sugared bun and buttered roll
The char lady knew the protocol.

Toast and crumpets were selling fast
Would the Rolos and KitKats last?
Past marketing and accounts
Closer and closer as the tension mounts.

She was nearly there with a squeak and rattle
The latest gossip and tittle-tattle.
She would never let you down
Not this time and not the next time around.

An inventor invented plant pots
That didn't need watering lots.
Just top 'em up once in a while
They're adaptable and versatile.

They're for the more discerning and astute
Bumper crops of roots, shoots and fruit.
And for other plants more ambiguous
Pampered, hardy and deciduous.

The pots are stacked in a stack
In threes or fours, it's not exact.
Vertical gardening stacked high
For seeding herbs or rare cacti.

And never let it be said he hadn't
Copyright © and a patent.
A registered trademark ® with an initial
In a circle so it's official.

A referee was keeping score
In a dogs v catchers tug-of-war.
The dogs were pulling in a pack
But the catchers were pulling back.

It was very much touch and go
In the dog v man to and fro.
Then there was some foul play
This could go either way.

The dogs on one end of the rope
Pulled the catchers down a muddy slope.
And between slippery, muddy slides
The dogs kept sliding and changing sides.

The dogs were up to dirty tricks
It was more fun than chasing sticks.
The referee declared the dogs had won
Then he barked and joined in the fun.

A ticket inspector was fully equipped
To check if a ticket's punched or clipped.
A ticket must be validated
Scrutinised and regulated.

The ticket inspector was alone again
Late at night and on an empty train.
Save for some dozing old codger
Could he be a fare dodger?

Was he a fare dodging cheat
With his feet up on a first-class seat?
He didn't look like a day tripper
A first-class passenger or big tipper.

Did he really belong in first class?
Did he have a dodgy ticket or expired pass?
Nodding off in the first-class section
The ticket inspector nudged his own reflection.

A miller unlocked the sails
While the wind was blowing gales.
And as soon as the sails were freed
They began to rise at high speed.

The sails were set and the sails were trimmed
The sails were raised by the wind.
Driving the grinding moans and groans
Of the rumbling grating stones.

On the mill on top of the hill
The sails wouldn't stop or stand still.
The sails would rise with creaks and clacks
To fill the miller's flour sacks.

Grain was ground and sacks were filled
Carts were loaded and flour was spilled.
And what's even more amazing
All of it was self-raising.

An optician suggested
A girl should get her eyes tested.
Looking over at the chart
She covered one eye and made a start.

a o b o a o is that an n?
Hold on, I'll start again.
a a o n d o i n o
No, no, I dunno.

I can see better if I squint
Can you give me a clue or hint?
a o a a o e It could be a g or an e
Are you allowed to help me?

This is so stressing
I think it's a z but I'm only guessing.
It looks like a z or an s
But that's only a wild guess.

An archaeologist found a Roman villa
With a mosaic and a marble pillar.
And a clear sign of Rome's long rule
Was a sunken bath or paddling pool.

Perhaps a place where geese would gaggle
To have a dip and doggie paddle.
He outlined the site with a tape
To dig a trench in the landscape.

The archaeologist would never begrudge
Working in the mud and sludge.
And he was quick to rush
To sweep and swipe with a toothbrush.

The sweeping and swiping alone
Would reveal much of this Roman home.
But after he's swept and swiped
He'd have a scrape that's what he liked.

A swan upper was swan upping when
He came across an elegant pen.
She was so graceful and such a cutie
He was overcome by her beauty.

He had a ring to put on
The dainty ankle of the swan.
But her mate had other ideas
They'd been together for many years.

The cob was strutting and was overheard
Saying, that bloke had better find his own bird.
He couldn't understand but he'd forgive 'er
And chuck that bloke in the river.

The swan upper was chucked and ducked
If he came back, he'd have him plucked.
But he calmed down after the feathers were flying
He couldn't blame a bloke for trying.

An office boy wanted to ask the new girl's name
But he didn't dare, what a shame.
Perhaps he could ask when she's alone
By herself and not on the phone.

But there might be trouble in the offin'
From some smart aleck computer boffin.
He was the office boy's pushy rival
In his new suit since her arrival.

He showed the girl his diploma
And asked her out once he'd shown 'er.
He told her about his potential
And asked her to keep it confidential.

The office boy was too shy
To wave at her or catch her eye.
Luckily, she preferred the shy type
Not a Clever Herbert in a pinstripe.

A new girl wouldn't tell her name
Until she made a boy play a game.
She was named after a flower or so she would say
And he was to take her a different one every day.

He needed to choose the right flower to win
He started with a rose just to begin.
He gave her a primrose and then a pink
A petunia, a lily and a pretty hyacinth.

A snowdrop, a buttercup and a bluebell
A poppy, a primrose but she still didn't tell.
Then a sprig of ivy, holly and mistletoe
It was worth a try, you never know.

But by now the boy was smitten
And left her a note that he'd written.
Roses are red violets are blue
Tell me your name and I'll marry you.

A gatherer was having a forage
For wild oats to make his porridge.
He had a bowl and a pan ready
For fresh milk to make his brekkie.

And in a clearing caked in mud
Stood a cow chewing the cud.
The gatherer had to think whether
He could get the two together.

The gatherer moved in gradual
Trying hard to look casual.
Chewing helps a cow think clearer.
But she thought he shouldn't come nearer.

With a flick of her tail and her ear
She hoped to make her position clear.
Keep your hands off me and stay downwind
Or you'll get pasteurised and semi-skimmed.

A weatherman was in the weather station
Expecting rain or precipitation.
He was predicting scattered showers
Throughout the night and early hours.

And a cold front was advancing fast
Bringing with it an icy blast.
Wet conditions could convert
Into high tides and a flood alert.

Downpours and cloudbursts could converge
To cause troughs and peaks to submerge.
That's before you factor in the wind chill
And the gale force winds' piercing shrill.

But waterlogged and drippy soaked
Could things be better than he'd hoped.
With fast spin and drip dried
He always looked on the bright side.

A digital nomad had her back to the door
In a café with the order she asked for.
Coffee smooth and hand roasted
Ground rich and quickly toasted.

She was unattached and traveling light
With a short let and a budget flight.
Nomad as the name implies
Means travelling without any ties.

She was sipping and tapping on her laptop
In her favourite Cook and Book shop.
But with a side order of extra fries
Cos only her luggage was downsized.

She was freely up and downloading
Web surfing and encoding.
A rolling stone gathers no boss
And that's no great loss.

A potter was making a potty
With wet clay squelchy sloppy.
She was up to her elbows in wet clay
Splashing water the potter's way.

And from the squelchy wallow
Rose the potty round and hollow.
And using her thumbs as she always did
She made a top or a lid.

And with a twist and a twiddle
She made a stripe around the middle.
She threw potties by the dozen
Then popped the lot in the oven.

The kiln blazed scorchy hot
To fix the glaze on the pot.
And get that sloppy potty
Ready for the first botty.

A sergeant was marching on the double
With his old kitbag and a nose for trouble.
In all weathers and without complaining
He was getting his lads through basic training.

With a chest full of medals and jutting chin
They had put all their trust in him.
Fighting dirty or fair
They'd follow him anywhere.

Whether over the top with one up the spout
Or bayonets fixed and pulling the pin out.
He would be the one to inspire
And always kept his cool under fire.

He wasn't one for chits or dockets
Guided missiles or firing rockets.
But surface-to-air or air-to-surface
They thanked him for his service.

A quantum mechanic had an equation
Up his sleeve for every occasion.
But even Albert Einstein despaired
Of ever finding $E=mc^2$.

In the beginning and Big Bang
Many a particle had a bump or prang.
Some were squashed and flattened
The Hadron Collider shows us what happened.

Particles veered and swerved
But some less so he observed.
Observation would be the key
To see how many got knocked silly.

He observed how particles spin and spun
Was there a Nobel Prize to be won?
Is the silly gene really a particle?
Was it too soon to publish his article?

A fish farmer peeped into a babbling brook
At a trout jumping with a knowing look.
Why was he looking up so happy
And leaping there so zippy-zappy?

In the cages where he kept his trout
They were always trying to break out.
Whenever they found a little hole, itty-bitty
Plans would be made by the escape committee.

They would get out one by one
To a new life on the run.
With a new identity and forged papers
They could join forces with other escapers.

The fish farmer couldn't be sure
Where he'd seen this one before.
Behind the lines and under cover
It would be hard to discover.

A scarecrow was scaring crows
In green pastures and meadows.
And he was always well dressed
In his flat cap and Sunday best.

He would always create a good impression
Without menacing gestures or aggression.
He wasn't one for harsh words
To scare away the little birds.

But there was one crow he couldn't scare
A caw cawing hoody that was always there.
Hovering like an uninvited guest
And pinching straw for his nest.

Pecking around high and low
With no regard for the scarecrow.
If he could put a stop to that
It would be a feather in his cap.

A bungee jumper took the plunge
100 feet towards a wet sponge.
Arms waving and legs spread
Just three thou betwixt sponge and head.

But he didn't always have such precision
It couldn't always be his best decision.
He could end with a wince or squirm
This might not be for him long-term.

He liked to think he could come within an inch
Without a blink or a flinch.
But his technique wasn't perfected
The ending could be unexpected.

If he couldn't always win
Perhaps it was time to chuck it in.
No more plungy jumpy hit or miss
He'd had enough of all this.

An ex-chess master had a lot to prove
And was about to make his first move.
Let battle rage let battle commence
Attack is the best form of defence.

But pieces were falling thick and fast
He was losing the battle and being outclassed.
A knight was jumping over the fallen and downed
And pieces were strewn across the battle ground.

Then the knight jumped over squares
Catching the queen unawares.
Running amuck and amok
The board was in for a shock.

The battle lines were drawn
When over the top went a little pawn.
The pawn slipped through the rank and file
To save his queen from exile.

A DJ had a late-night show
On the local radio.
The DJ played all the hits
And never talked over the best bits.

Speaking in a DJ voice
Hushed and husky was an easy choice.
Playing the favourites of the guests
And taking phone-ins and requests.

With a spin on the turntable
And a plug for the record label.
And when all that was done
It was time for the number one.

Some were climbing and some were dropping
Some were hitting and some were flopping.
They can't all be top of the pops
There are drops and there are flops.

An engraver was engraving
On an ID bracelet he'd been saving.
For someone special if he ever reveals
His plans and how he feels.

He engraved a name on the bracelet
Catherine's name was his favourite.
And he gave it an extra polish and buff
For Catherine to tuck under her cuff.

Now everyone would know
If she ever let it show.
But Catherine never revealed
The bracelet she concealed.

Hidden beneath its cover of cotton
Out of sight and then forgotten.
Now lying abandoned in an old oak chest
On his buttonhole and her wedding dress.

A trapper set a snappy-trap
During a wintery cold snap.
To trap a white toothy-snapper
It'd take a brave winter trapper.

Head bowed through blizzard's blow
Danced the Trapper deep in snow.
For only trappers bonkers and crackers
Would go to trap toothy-snappers.

Through the mist blurry and swirly
Came a toothy-snapper white and furry.
Stepping over traps snappy-catchy
Came the Trapper brave but batty.

With traps and toothy-snapper all in place
Trapper and snapper came face to face.
Snapper and trapper side stepping as one
The winter two-step could be fun.

A prospector had an itch
To stake a claim and strike it rich.
But he had a long way to go
To reach the hills and plateaux.

He loaded his mule and packed his pony
So, his mule wouldn't get lonely.
And spoke to them in whispers
Spat out dust and scratched his whiskers.

He took a canteen of water and refills
It's thirsty work in them thar hills.
And snake oil for snake bite
Leaving early before it got light.

He headed out making tracks
With a spade, a shovel and pickaxe.
Making tracks with every tool
Went the prospector, pony and mule.

A claim jumper saw his best chance
To jump a claim and do the gold dance.
He saw a prospector had filed a claim
And left a marker, which is much the same.

A prospector left some rocks flat and piled
To show the claim was staked and filed.
And he mined, panned and dug it
Looking for gold dust or a nugget.

The claim jumper used a telescope
To keep an eye out for the prospector's approach.
But the prospector was in no rush
And stepped lightly through the sagebrush.

With binoculars and holding his mule's tale
The prospector came closer along the trail.
And was trying to think whether or not
He'd remembered to pack his buckshot.

A clockmaker looked a clock in the face
And saw there were parts to replace.
The winder was very rare
But luckily, he had a spare.

He had every part in stock
To repair any kind of clock.
Dials with big and little hands
Winders, springs and even wrist bands.

With his fiddly fingers wheels and tweezers
Trembly assemblies and incy squeezers.
And peepy-squinty magnifiers
Pincers and tiny screwdrivers.

With dinky spanners and a wrench
For twists and turns on his workbench.
He was fixing cuckoos, alarms and chimes
For tea, supper and bedtimes.

A tree surgeon had a branch to trim
And crawled out on a limb.
In his right hand he carried a lopper
And in his left his trusty chopper.

Where it was thickest
He moved the quickest.
And straddled, shuffled and chopped
And where it was thinnest he lopped.

With skill and precision
He made his incision.
And continued to prune and lop
With a swing swipe and chop.

He swiped and sliced but in the treetop
The secret is knowing when to stop.
The trunk was reduced to a coppiced clump
And whittled away to a splintered stump.

A tennis ace was making a comeback
Tossed up a ball and gave it a whack.
The umpire called for new balls
Ace tucked them in her smalls.

Her whack was called out
But she had a nagging doubt?
The umpire was approached and confronted
Then she rallied, served and grunted.

She served, volleyed and somersaulted
Over the net and double faulted.
The umpire called let!
It wasn't over yet.

She was attacking on all fronts
With sobs, lobs and grunts.
Balls were smashed and backhanded
There's no telling where they landed.

A pirate in his eyepatch and bandana
Sauntered on deck in a jaunty manner.
Cannons fired and decks shook
The pirate kept an eye out for a look.

Guns blasted louder and louder
With fuses, smoke and gunpowder.
Ducking cannon balls, muck and shot
The pirate bravely shrugged off the lot.

The swashbuckler was in hot pursuit
Of booty, treasure and galleon's loot.
The pirate's sloop was much faster
Than the bulky galleon he was after.

But then he was overpowered and outnumbered
And gave up the doubloons that he'd plundered.
He walked the plank, dropped and swum
Then it was time for tea and tell his mum.

A trawlerman was stowing his catch
A seagull was peeking down the hatch.
Fish are what the seagull was seeking
With its squawking, shrieking and peeking.

The trawlerman would trawl and haul
To squawks and shrills of birdcall.
Fish were hauled and stowed
And slid and hid down the hold.

Seagull had a clever technique
For snatching fish with its beak.
The seagull would wait its chance
To begin a squawky fishy dance.

And when the trawlerman was distracted
With the attention the dancing attracted.
Fish would slide down its gullet
Sardines, sprat and grey mullet.

A washerwoman with thumps and thuds
Was dunking washing in soapy suds.
With soapy bubbles all around her
She shook in more washing powder.

Washing and scrubbing rub-a-dub-dub
On the washboard of her washtub.
Then she stopped the soaking and sploshing
To rinse and wring and take out the washing.

With bubbles bursting up her nose
She wrung out the drippy clothes.
Then her washing was swung and flung
On the line where it clung and hung.

Waving and blowing with drippy drips
And flappy waves like sails on ships.
Waves and flaps hung out together
Come rain or shine or drying weather.

A planner found potholes in the road
And ordered filler by the truckload.
New potholes on the hard shoulder
And even more that were older.

One was filled as the planner planned
With a dash of cement and a shovel of sand.
A sprinkling of gravel and a dab of tar
Poured and flattened as pancakes are.

Ready for the traffic to batter
And flatten it even flatter.
The planner whisked up the mixture
Thick and lumpy for the fixture.

Crushed and stuffed and trodden in
But the filler would soon wear thin.
Another started to come apart
That's the way sinkholes start.

An eloper held the ladder steady
His fiancé would soon be ready.
She'd climb out the widow as rehearsed
On the stroke of midnight and feet first.

Nothing would keep them apart
All he needed was a head start.
The eloper would arrive with his intended
Where Scotland began and England ended.

With his radio and a singsong
If music be the food of love, play on.
Lovestruck and Shakespeare quoted
On he drove mop haired and duffle coated.

Racing along in his little car
Her dad behind with his Jag and cigar.
Not sheep on the road nor the unforeseen
Would stop him getting to Gretna Green.

A mime artist could be a balloon blower
A flower sniffer or a knife thrower.
If the knives didn't really exist
It wouldn't matter if he missed.

Or he could be a golfer with a hole in one
Or a boxer who could have been someone.
And walking a tightrope across rooftops
It wouldn't matter if he drops.

And as quiet as a little mouse
He could vacuum a whole house.
Or play a big didgeridoo
It wouldn't matter if he sucked or blew.

He could ride a bike or roller skate
Conduct an orchestra or swing on a gate.
Finish a race with a burst
It wouldn't matter who comes first?

A clergyman was fishing a chalk stream
Moving quietly, silently in the extreme.
He was fly fishing for trout
Reeling in and casting out.

He made the flies with great care
Out of bird feathers and horsehair.
He tied on a Chucklewing
And cast it with a springy swing.

Casting line out of town
He caught a rainbow and a brown.
Weighing in at two pounds at least
And quickly visited by the priest.

Then in the nave below the vault
He cooked the fish that he caught.
He poached the rainbow and the brown
Shh! Keep your voice down.

Thank you for reading.

If you enjoyed Ponytail Tales, please consider leaving a short review on Amazon. It helps other readers discover the book and supports future Ponytail adventures.

Thank you

Barry.

Printed in Dunstable, United Kingdom

67143080R00178